Evidence for God
from Physics and Philosophy

The University of Dallas Aquinas Lectures
are published in cooperation with
St. Augustine's Press.

Evidence for God
from Physics and Philosophy
Extending the Legacy of Monsignor Georges Lemaître and St. Thomas Aquinas

ROBERT J. SPITZER, S.J.

Foreword
by
Christopher V. Mirus

ST. AUGUSTINE'S PRESS
South Bend, Indiana

Manufactured in the United States of America.

1 2 3 4 5 6   20 19 18 17 16 15

Library of Congress Cataloging in Publication Data
Spitzer, Robert J., 1952–
Evidence for God from physics and philosophy: extending the legacy of Monsignor Georges Lemaître and St. Thomas Aquinas / Robert J. Spitzer, S.J. ; foreword by Christopher V. Mirus. – 1st [edition].
pages cm. – (The University of Dallas Aquinas lectures)
Includes bibliographical references.
ISBN 978-1-58731-239-7 (clothbound: alk. paper) 1. God (Christianity) 2. God – Proof. 3. Physics – Religious aspects – Christianity. 4. Philosophical theology. 5. Lemaître, Georges, 1894–1966.
6. Thomas, Aquinas, Saint, 1225?–1274. 7. Dawkins, Richard, 1941– I. Title.
BT103.S6865 2010
261.5'5 – dc23   2014044298

St. Augustine's Press
www.staugustine.net

Table of Contents

Foreword

The natural sciences are, of course, human endeavors, driven and shaped by human aspirations. Yet among the branches of human inquiry, only mathematics aspires to a more thorough forgetfulness of self. Natural scientists are immersed in an intellectual practice that, for all its dependence on funding and ambition, profit and application, still rewards those who aspire to take natural realities on their own relatively impersonal terms. In the humanities and the human sciences, by contrast, intellectual excellence requires greater personal engagement. When our subject matter is human—or, for that matter, divine—having one's heart in the right place counts for more, mere excellence of method for less. Without minimizing the human capacity for stubbornness, error, and plain failure to see the point—which of course affect every inquiry—we can say that studying nature tends to be more straightforward than studying man or God.

This straightforwardness, which we sometimes call "objectivity," gives natural science a certain prestige. We often see natural science and its practitioners as occupying a kind of sanctuary, removed from the demands and uncertainty of human life as a whole. When, therefore, science appears to say something that bears on the human or the divine, we are quick to listen. We don't want to miss an opportunity to straighten out and clarify contentious matters by appealing, as it were, to an impartial judge. To be sure, we tend to listen more assiduously when the judge seems likely to decide in our favor. We hope, however—with good reason—that we shall not have to win an appeal against science.

In this book—an expanded version of his 2014 University of Dallas Aquinas Lecture—Fr. Robert Spitzer reflects on two important conclusions of theoretical physics. First, the universe as we know it began billions of years ago with an unimaginably powerful physical event, the "Big Bang." Second, the universe as we know it is much more orderly than we have any right to expect. Both conclusions, Fr. Spitzer argues, ought to point philosophical reflection toward God. In response to an objection formulated by Richard Dawkins, Fr. Spitzer adds a third and more thoroughly philosophical argument drawn from the writings of St. Thomas Aquinas.

These arguments are challenging. On one hand, a little more than two hundred years ago it would have seemed paradoxical in the extreme to craft an argument for the existence of a creator based on an account of cosmic history so thoroughly different from the creation narrative of Genesis. Even today, many believers remain perplexed by science's propensity to combine extraordinary grandeur of vision with complete disregard for the biblical account. On the other hand, the idea that science might provide evidence for any sort of god—biblical or otherwise—seems just as paradoxical to many. Surely, the whole point of science is to do away with such supernatural explanations! A third group of readers, less unsettled by the general thrust of Fr. Spitzer's arguments, may nevertheless find themselves wondering about their competence to judge the arguments' success, or about how much trust should be placed in scientific and philosophical arguments—for or against—

concerning what seem ultimately to be matters of faith.

Now given the human tendency to find in science the triumphant vindication of what one already knows, and given that we are, in fact, dealing with matters of faith, Fr. Spitzer's arguments surely call for a careful, reflective reading. We can find some good advice for our reading in a much older text that also takes up the existence of God: St. Augustine's *On Free Choice of the Will*. In this fictional dialogue between himself and a young man named Evodius, Augustine urges us to take up a paradoxical position when seeking knowledge of God. He insists that no one can understand God without faith; as the prophet Isaiah says, "Unless you believe, you shall not understand" (Is 7:9, LXX). Yet he also suggests that if we do wish to understand, then we must approach God's existence as if we were not already convinced (see *On Free Choice of the Will*, I.2, II.2). These two requirements seem incompatible.

The solution to Augustine's paradox is found in his conviction that "what we seek at God's bidding we shall find when he himself shows us" (ibid., II.2.19). Reason—which is, Augustine believes, God's own light within the human soul—can indeed reveal the existence, power, and wisdom of God. It does so, however, only when we are willing to loosen our grip on the very thing we wish to possess. God is not to be found by squeezing harder and harder, with our own meager strength, the small intimations of his glory that we have already received. Such a tightening of our grip is not so much an effort to find God as the nervous complacency of those who believe he is already theirs, signed, sealed, and delivered.

Augustine wishes Evodius to arrive at a more mature faith. In particular, he wants him to discover God not only in the Scriptures—that is, in the religious experience of others—but within his own soul. (Compare II.2.14–15 with the approach to God taken in II.3–16.) Far from belittling Scripture, Augustine is convinced that Evodius will truly understand the inspired texts only when he discovers that God is intimately present within himself too. Paradoxically, to arrive at this mature understanding Evodius must have the faith to step away from what he thinks he knows. Rather than clinging possessively to what he already believes, he must let God himself show him what he wishes to understand.

Strangely enough, it might seem, Augustine's faith-filled assertion that God himself will show us what we seek is followed immediately by a long, provocative, philosophical argument for the existence of God. Augustine did not, then, consider faith in God's willingness to reveal himself an excuse for passivity. The argument he presents, moreover, is based in large part on the ideas of thinkers unfamiliar with the Christian Scriptures. This combination of intellectual ambition with the humility to learn from others was essential to his extraordinary openness to being taught by God.

Whether we are looking for God in the human soul or in the structure and origin of the physical universe—and for Augustine, at any rate, the two inquiries are closely connected—Augustine's advice and example are sound. I would venture to say that in a certain respect, they are as sound for the atheist as for the believer. We are unlikely to grasp the existence or nonexistence of God, at least with any understanding, as long as we are fixated on what we think we already know. Conviction without daring is no conviction; daring without an eye for the unexpected is no daring. For the believer specifically, willingness to be surprised by God stands at the heart of authentic faith.

Augustine's argument coaxed Evodius away from his easy security in the inspired word into the majestic yet challenging space of the human heart. In much the same way, Fr. Spitzer's arguments draw us into the majestic yet challenging space of the physical world, offering a new and richer context for the scriptural doctrine of creation. Like Augustine's, his arguments draw on important and challenging contemporary ideas to craft a provocative argument for the existence of God—an argument that, like Augustine's, challenges both those who wish to rely on scriptural faith alone and those who reject faith altogether.

Fr. Spitzer's argument is also challenging in that, like the human soul, nature so often appears to obscure God rather than revealing him. In fact, Augustine's dialogue is ultimately concerned with human freedom and with the problem of evil. That is, Augustine searched for God within the human soul despite his awareness that "more tortuous than anything is the human heart, beyond remedy; who can understand it?" (Jer 17:9). Like the study of the human heart, the study of nature can challenge our faith.

Augustine understood, however, that the deeper and more mature our faith, the readier we will be to leave the security of what we think we know, so that God himself may show us what we truly seek.

Like Augustine's, therefore, Fr. Spitzer's arguments are best assessed through prayerful study and reflection. They should not be read as painless, triumphant victories over scientific atheism, but as invitations to let God show us what he himself wants us to understand—what his creation is meant to reveal. This was also, of course, the approach of St. Thomas himself. Such an approach provides us with the freedom to take each argument—indeed, to take science or philosophy itself—on its own terms, to assess its strengths and weaknesses through reflection and further study, and, in short, to learn from it as much as we can.

Christopher V. Mirus
August 19, 2014

Introduction

I write this essay in the spirit of St. Thomas
Aquinas, acknowledging that much of the discussion in it is taken from contemporary physics and
cosmology with which he was not familiar. Nevertheless, St. Thomas plays a prominent role in responding to the philosophical objections of a
well-known naturalistic skeptic, Richard Dawkins
(see below section VII), and he set the stage for
exploring the intersection of faith and science in
the *Summa contra gentiles* when he declared:

> Although the truth of the Christian faith
> which we have discussed surpasses the
> capacity of the reason, nevertheless that
> truth that the human reason is naturally
> endowed to know cannot be opposed to
> the truth of the Christian faith. For that
> with which the human reason is naturally

> endowed is clearly most true; so much so,
> that it is impossible for us to think of
> such truths as false. Nor is it permissible
> to believe as false that which we hold by
> faith, since this is confirmed in a way that
> is so clearly divine.[1]

The natural sciences (and philosophical reflection upon them) have been an integral part of the Catholic intellectual tradition since the time of the Copernican revolution. Indeed, Catholic priests and clerics played a central role in the development of natural science; for example, Nicolaus Copernicus (1473–1543, the originator of the heliocentric universe and its mathematical justification) was a Catholic cleric.[2] Nicolas Steno (1638–1686, a Catholic Danish bishop) is acknowledged to be one of the founders of modern stratigraphy and geology.[3] The Augustinian monk and abbot Gregor Mendel (1822–1884) is

1 Thomas Aquinas, *Summa contra gentiles*, Book I, chap. 7, section 1.
2 Copernicus was a devout Catholic who took minor orders as a Catholic cleric and was a canon lawyer within the Catholic Church, but he did not proceed to ordination as a priest. See Armitage 1990.
3 See Hansen 2009.

acknowledged to be the founder of modern genetics.[4] As will be discussed below, Monsignor Georges Lemaître (a Belgian priest and colleague of Albert Einstein) is acknowledged to be the founder of contemporary cosmology (the Big Bang theory, in 1927).[5] There are many other Catholic clerics who were integrally involved in the foundation and development of the natural sciences.

Some have contended that the Catholic Church manifested an "antiscientific attitude" during the controversy with Galileo, but the controversy was not about the veracity of scientific method or its seeming heliocentric conclusion. The Jesuits of the Roman College helped Galileo to confirm mathematically his version of the

4 See Henig 2000.
5 Although Father Lemaître was too humble to assert the primacy of his discovery over that of Edwin Hubble (two years later), Lemaître is widely acknowledged today to be the true founder of the Big Bang theory—one of the most rigorously established theories in contemporary physics. The theory has undergone many modifications since the time of Father Lemaître (1927), but the general theory of the expanding universe remains the same. See Livio 2011 and Plotner 2011.

heliocentric theory and considered him to be an esteemed colleague and friend. The relationship broke down only when Galileo disobeyed the pope about announcing the heliocentric universe as *fact* (before adequate astronomical observations could be made to confirm the theory through a technique called "stellar parallax").[6] He exacerbated the strained relationship when he called the pope and the Jesuits "fools" because of their reservation. The Catholic Church has never been "anti-science," but rather creatively instrumental in its development, making science to be an integral part of its intellectual tradition.

6   The stellar parallax technique is essential to confirming the earth's movement around the sun, but astronomical observations of distant stars were not accurate enough to confirm the earth's movement relative to the sun until over 200 years after Galileo—in 1839, when it was calculated by Friedrich Bessel. The pope and the Jesuits were justified in asking Galileo not to claim his theory as fact until this critical astronomical observation had been made. Unfortunately, he chose not to do so, and the controversy (and breakdown of a long-standing collegial relationship) began. See Wallace 1984 and DeMarco 1986, pp. 23–51 and 53–59.

Introduction

An additional point should be made at the outset: contemporary physics cannot avoid philosophical analysis because its conclusions have pushed into the domain of metaphysics. In section I, we will discuss how the conclusions of contemporary cosmology need clarification from philosophy to show the proper limits and horizons of its method. In section V, we will see how conclusions of contemporary cosmology (from evidence of a beginning of physical reality) inevitably lead into the domain of metaphysics. In section VII, we will see how a Thomistic metaphysical argument for God can best respond to the objections of Richard Dawkins in his attempt to discount supernatural design. In all of these cases, the physicists (and their metaphysical theories) could have avoided both misleading and false conclusions with some very simple, well-known principles of logic and philosophical analysis. I hope this essay will bring together the best of both disciplines to reveal the truth that both St. Thomas Aquinas and Monsignor Georges Lemaître believed and sought—a truth commensurate with both faith and reason.

I.

Physical and Metaphysical Method: Can Science Indicate Creation?

We should begin by clarifying what science can really tell us about a beginning of the universe and supernatural causation. First, unlike philosophy and metaphysics, science cannot *deductively* prove a creation or God. Natural science deals with the physical universe and with the regularities which we call "laws of nature" that are obeyed by the phenomena within that universe. But God is not an object or phenomenon or regularity within the physical universe, so science cannot not say anything about God.

Moreover, science is an empirical and inductive discipline. As such, science cannot be certain that it has considered all possible data relevant to a complete explanation of particular physical phenomena or the universe itself. It must always remain open to new data and discoveries that could alter its explanation of particular phenomena and the universe. This can be seen quite clearly in the movement from the Newtonian view of the universe to the Einsteinian one, or from the geocentric Ptolemaic view of the solar system to the heliocentric Copernican one.

So what *can* science tell us? It can identify, aggregate, and synthesize evidence indicating the finitude of past time in the universe (as we currently know it to be and conceive it could be). Science can also identify the exceedingly high improbability of the random occurrence of conditions necessary to sustain life in the universe (as we currently know it to be and conceive it could be). Although scientific conclusions are subject to change in the light of new data, we should not let this possibility cause us to discount unnecessarily the validity of long-standing, persistent, rigorously established theories. If we did this, we might discount the majority of all scientific theories. Thus, it is reasonable and responsible to attribute qualified truth value to such theories until such time as new data requires them to be modified.

The arguments that suggest the finitude of past time—in other words, that time had a beginning—are basically of two types: (a) arguments about the possible geometries of space-time and (b) arguments based on the Second Law of Thermodynamics (entropy). Although the arguments we shall give may conceivably have loopholes, in the sense that cosmological models or scenarios may be found in the future to which these arguments do not apply, their persistence and applicability to a large number of existing cosmological models gives them respectable probative force. Until such time as they are shown to be invalid or inapplicable to empirically verifiable characteristics of our universe, they should be considered as justifying the conclusion that it is at least probable that the universe had a beginning.

When we speak of a beginning (a point prior to which there is no physical reality), we stand at the threshold of metaphysics (beyond physics). Although science cannot be validly used to prove a metaphysical claim (such as, "a Creator or God exists"), it can be used (with the qualifications mentioned above) to maintain as highly probable a limit to physical reality (such as a beginning). This *scientific* evidence for a beginning can be combined with a *metaphysical* premise (such as "from nothing, only nothing comes") to render a *metaphysical* conclusion that there must be *something* beyond physical reality which caused physical reality to exist (that is, a transcendent cause).

There are other indications of supernatural causation arising out of contemporary cosmology besides the implications of a beginning—namely, the occurrence of several cosmological conditions essential for the development and sustenance of any life form—that seem at least to be highly improbable. These seemingly highly improbable conditions (which are sometimes called "cosmic coincidences" or "anthropic coincidences") imply an element of supernatural fine-tuning if no satisfactory naturalistic explanation can be found for them.

The existence of a Creator does not rest on scientific cosmological evidence alone. There are sufficient rational grounds to affirm the existence of a Creator without modern science (see section VII).[7] Nevertheless, the purely philosophical and

7   See also the three proofs in Spitzer 2010(a), chaps. 3–5.

metaphysical arguments and the arguments based on the findings of modern science complement and corroborate each other. This complementarity and corroboration constitute a network of evidence. John Henry Newman termed such a network of evidence an "informal inference," that is, reaching a conclusion by considering the accumulation of converging independently probable data sets. This allows for possible modification of one or more of the sets without significantly changing the general conclusion (see section VIII).

Using the foregoing methodological considerations as a foundation, we may now respond to three naturalistic claims that have become widely accepted in popular culture:

1. Science can and has disproven the existence of a Creator.

2. Science currently knows everything about the universe sufficient to conclude that the universe does not need a Creator.

3. Science can give no evidence for a transcendent Creator.

Let us begin with the first naturalistic claim (according to which science can disprove a Creator). This claim is completely beyond the domain of science, because scientific evidence must be observational (whether it be directly observed, measured, inferred from an experiment, etc.). This observational evidence is limited to our universe (and even to our event horizon within the universe). However, a *transcendent* Creator would have to be beyond the confines of our observational data, and so science cannot *disprove* the existence of a transcendent Creator. An elaboration of the problem will make this clear. It is much more difficult to disprove something by means of observation than to prove it. For example, if I want to prove the existence of an alien, I need to see only one; however, if I wish to disprove the existence of aliens by observational method, I would have to observe everything that there is to observe in the universe, know with certainty that all realities within the universe come within my purview and observational powers, and then notice that it is not there. Thus, *disproving* by means of observation requires a comprehensive search and infallible certitude that all realities can be observed by the observer (which certainly cannot be known through observation!). The problem becomes even worse when we are speaking about a reality outside of the observable universe (such as a transcendent Creator, or God). This would entail observing everything there is to observe *outside* the universe, knowing that all realities outside the universe are in fact observable, and noticing that it is not there. This is evidently an impossible task—enough said.

Let us turn to the second naturalistic claim—namely that science now knows enough about the universe to know with certainty that the universe does not need a Creator.[8] This contention cannot be the case today or at any other time in the future, because science is an *inductive* discipline. This means that science proceeds from specific observational data to theories that coherently unify this data. Sometimes scientists are able to formulate "rigorously established" theories that are corroborated by multiple different data sets and a convergence of the mathematics intrinsic to those data sets (such as the Big Bang theory). Though rigorously established theories should be considered to indicate truth, they can never be known with infallible certitude, because scientists can

8   See the discussion on the *Larry King Show* between Stephen Hawking, Leonard Mlodinow, Deepak Chopra, and Fr. Robert Spitzer (http://www.youtube.com/watch?v=9AdKEHzmqxA). This is Hawking's and Mlodinow's contention.

never know what they do not know until they have discovered it. Theories are not theorems (proofs); they are only coherent unifications of *currently available* data (observations). Thus, scientists can never know whether their theories are completely explanatory (they cannot, that is, know that there are no data in the universe unaccounted for). Inasmuch as the completeness of a theory cannot be known by observational evidence, it cannot be known by science, and for this reason science must remain open to further discoveries—always.[9] Therefore, science can never know with certainty that the universe does not need a Creator, because it cannot know with certainty that it has accounted for all data in the

9   The idea that M Theory is perfectly explanatory is doubly fallacious. Although M Theory *can* show how an eleven-dimensional vibrating string configuration could give rise to all the kinds and spins of particles, no scientist can know that M Theory exhausts the whole of physical reality (for the reasons mentioned above). There is a second problem with this contention—namely, that we do not currently have any evidence for string theory (or M Theory), and it looks as if these theories may be inapplicable to some aspects of the observable universe. See Dine 2004; see Gordon 2010.

universe affecting the answer to this question. Furthermore, this claim conflicts directly with the evidence for a creation of the universe discussed in the third claim.

We proceed finally to the third naturalistic claim—namely, that science can give no evidence for a transcendent reality (such as a Creator or God). At first it might seem that if science *cannot* give evidence against a Creator, then it should not be able to give evidence for a Creator. However, recall that it is much easier to prove something with observational evidence than to disprove it, because disproving requires observing everything that is real, and noticing that a hypothetical entity is not there. Accomplishing this task for an entity outside the universe (outside of our observational horizon) is impossible. However, if one could show that the universe (and even physical reality itself) cannot explain its own existence, then it would be possible to give evidence for a reality beyond the universe. So is there any evidence *within* the universe that shows that the universe cannot explain itself? As a matter of fact there is: a finite limit to past time or what is commonly called "a beginning." As I have noted, if science could show through observational evidence that the universe (and even physical reality itself) must have a beginning, then this datum could be combined with a metaphysical premise (that physical reality was absolutely nothing before the beginning) to show that the universe could not have moved itself from nothing to something before the beginning. This would require a transcendent Creator to move physical reality from nothing to something at the beginning. Well then, can science give evidence for a beginning of the universe, the beginning of a multiverse, and even the beginning of physical reality itself? We now proceed to sections II through IV for that answer.

II.

Georges Lemaître, the Big Bang Theory, and the Modern Universe

Monsignor Georges Lemaître, a Catholic priest, noted cosmologist, and colleague of Einstein's, formulated the Big Bang theory in 1927.[10] As I will explain in section III, Lemaître ingeniously solved the problem of how the recessional velocities of distant galaxies could be greater than those of nearer galaxies. The idea was really quite radical—so much so that Einstein, though impressed with Lemaître's mathematics, rejected it at first. Lemaître theorized that galaxies were not moving

---

10   Mario Livio 2011.

in fixed Euclidean space, but rather that the space between the galaxies was stretching and growing, analogous to a balloon being inflated. Think for a moment about a balloon with many dots on it, and liken the elastic of the balloon to the spatial manifold (spatial field) and the dots on the balloon to galaxies. Now circle one of the dots on the balloon, and call it the Milky Way (our galaxy), and begin blowing up the balloon. Notice that every time you exhale into the balloon and stretch the elastic more, the farther dots from us expand more than the nearer dots. Why did the farther dots move farther away from us than the nearer dots? Because there was more space—more balloon—between them and us (than between the nearer galaxies and us). So, Lemaître reasoned that the more space there was to stretch and grow, the more stretching and growing would occur, and the more stretching and growing that occurred, the greater the recessional velocity (the distance a galaxy moves away from us per unit time) would be.

Lemaître knew that Einstein's General Theory of Relativity allowed not only for the spatial field to have a variable geometry (such as a curved geometrical configuration surrounding dense fields of mass-energy), but also for space to stretch and grow like the expansion of a balloon. He showed with great mathematical precision that the expansion of the universe as a whole was the best explanation of the recessional velocities of distant galaxies, but his conclusion was so radical that Einstein and others found it difficult to accept. Furthermore, it had the consequence that the universe may have had a beginning (a creation), which was a true departure from previous scientific assumptions. Why does Lemaître's theory have such a consequence? If the universe truly is expanding as a whole (irrespective of whether it expands uniformly like a balloon or not) it must have been less expanded in the past, and even less expanded as we go further back into the past. Today there is only a finite distance between galaxies, and so we know that the universe could not have been expanding forever in the past. All of the points must have been arbitrarily close to one another at some time *in the finite past*. If the Big Bang[11] marks the initial expansion of the

---

11 Fr. Georges Lemaître did not use the term "Big Bang," but rather spoke of "the Theory of the Primeval Atom." Sir Fred Hoyle (when he was in his atheistic

universe, then it could be the *beginning* of the universe. We have very good evidence today that this event occurred about 13.8 billion years ago (plus or minus 100,000,000 years).

Nothing like this had ever been considered in the natural sciences before Fr. Lemaître formulated his theory. Aristotle and St. Thomas Aquinas believed that the evidence of reason could not establish a beginning of time, and so natural philosophy would have to assume the eternity of the universe. St. Thomas thought that the finitude of time in the universe could only be known through the revelation of God (requiring faith). Sir Isaac Newton made the same assumption, and so did his followers, right up to the time of Fr. Lemaître. Although Lemaître did not prove that the Big Bang was the beginning of the universe, his theory implied that it could be, and this radically changed the intellectual landscape (and horizon) of the natural sciences. Lemaître put it this way:

> We can compare space-time to an open,
> conic cup. ... The bottom of the cup is
> the origin of atomic disintegration; it is

phase) sneeringly dubbed Lemaître's theory "the Big Bang" to trivialize and insult it.

> the first instant at the bottom of space-
> time, the now which has no yesterday
> because, yesterday, there was no
> space.[12]

Lemaître's theory was first confirmed two years later by Edwin Hubble's survey of the heavens at Mt. Wilson Observatory, in which he showed through a well-known technique called red-shifting that more distant galaxies are indeed moving away from our galaxy faster than those nearer to us. Hubble invited Einstein to Mt. Wilson to check the results, which apparently caused him to change his mind. When Einstein and Lemaître co-presented at a conference at Mt. Wilson in 1933, Einstein reputedly said, "This is the most beautiful and satisfactory explanation of creation to which I have ever listened."[13] Since that time, Lemaître's theory has been confirmed in a variety of different ways, making it one of the most comprehensive and rigorously established theories in contemporary cosmology.

12 Lemaître 1950, p. 133.
13 Topper 2013, p. 175 and also in *New York Times* 01/02/2005: "Even Einstein Had His Days Off" (http://www.nytimes.com/2005/01/02/opinion/02sing h.html).

After Hubble's confirmation through the red-shifts detected in his survey of the heavens, Arno Penzias and Robert Wilson made another remarkable confirmation in 1965 through a very different approach. They inadvertently discovered a 2.7-degree Kelvin, uniformly distributed radiation throughout the universe that could have occurred only at a very early, cosmos-wide event (the Big Bang and its immediate aftermath).[14] They received the Nobel Prize for this discovery in 1978. The Big Bang was subsequently confirmed by data from the cosmic background explorer satellites (COBE) #1 and #2,[15] the Wilkinson Microwave Anisotropy Probe (WMAP),[16] and very recently by the Planck Satellite.[17] These confirmations verify Fr. Lemaître's general concept of the Big Bang, and add consider-

14 Penzias and Wilson 1965, pp. 419–21.
15 NASA Report on the Findings of the COBE Satellites (http://lambda.gsfc.nasa.gov/product/cobe/).
16 NASA press conference with NASA Director Charles Bennett on data from the WMAP Satellite 2008 (http://www.space.com/scienceastronomy/map_discovery_030211).
17 NASA press conferences on Planck Satellite 2013 (http://www.nasa.gov/planck and http://www.nasa.gov/mission_pages/planck/news/planck20130321.html).

ably more to it—such as the possibility of quantum gravity, inflationary theory, dark matter, and dark energy (which will be described briefly).

So what do physicists think happened 13.8 billion years ago? It seems that our universe took a quantum cosmological form in which all four forces (the electromagnetic force, the strong nuclear force, the weak force, and the gravitational force—in a quantized form) were completely unified, and then exploded. At that moment the space-time manifold came into existence and energy emerged in it (in a fashion explicable by Einstein's General Theory of Relativity). The strong nuclear force separated from the electroweak force, and then the weak force separated from the electromagnetic force, which then moved through a Higgs field, slowing it down to produce the rest mass of particles (such as protons and neutrons) that make up the visible constituents of the universe. A plasma era ensued, followed by stellar nucleosynthesis and galactic formation, eventually giving rise to planets—and even to some very special planets similar to the Earth.[18]

18 The current estimate of such special planets in the Milky Way is approximately 40 billion according to

The observable universe appears to have approximately 10^{55} kilograms of visible matter, about five times more dark matter (25% of the universe)[19] and considerably more dark energy (about 70% of the universe).[20] The visible and dark matter

researchers Erik Petigura and Geoffrey Marcy of the University of California, Berkeley, along with Andrew Howard of the University of Hawaii, using data from the Kepler Satellite (designed to detect planets in our galaxy and beyond); see NPR news report, November 2013: "Just How Many Earth-like Planets are Out There?" (http://www.npr.org/2013/11/05/242991030 /galaxy-quest-just-how-many-earth-like-planets-are-out-there). Does life exist on any of these planets? Nobody knows. There is a possibility that some of these planets may be able to sustain life, and therefore may have life, but current investigations (such as those carried out by the Mars Curiosity Rover) have not found any data to support this.

19 Dark matter does not emit or absorb light or heat, so it is not detectable by traditional methods. It is currently thought to take the form of very fine particles that interact with the space-time manifold in the same way as visible matter (causing an increased curvature of the manifold in proportion to its density). It is what keeps the galaxies of the observable universe from flying apart (in the accelerated fashion of the space between the galaxies).

20 Dark energy is quite different from dark matter.

is distributed in 10^{22} stars (and accompanying planets) within 10^{11} galaxies. The galaxies maintain their volume because of visible matter, dark matter, and a giant black hole in their centers. However, the space between the galaxies is stretching at an accelerated rate (inflating) because of dark energy. It is highly unlikely that the universe will collapse in the future (in a big crunch followed by a bounce), because it is probable that flat geometry and dark energy will cause it to expand indefinitely. Therefore, the universe will reach a point of either a "big freeze" (in which the gases necessary for star formation will be exhausted, and all formed stars will use up their supply of gases) or "heat death" (in which the universe reaches maximum entropy) at a finite time in the future (somewhere between 1 trillion and 100 trillion years from now).

Instead of interacting with the space-time manifold in a way that causes contraction, it causes repulsion. It seems to have a field-like dimensionality that causes the space-time manifold to stretch and grow at an accelerated rate, causing the phenomenon known as inflation. There is some convincing evidence of inflation from the Planck Satellite and other observations, and the best current explanation for this inflation is dark energy.

This brings us to three central questions: Was the Big Bang the beginning of our universe? Does our universe exhaust the whole of physical reality (or is there some dimension of physical reality beyond our universe)? If physical reality does extend beyond our universe, must it have a beginning? Quantum gravity[21] and inflation theory[22]

21 Quantum gravity is a hypothetical field of physics that tries to describe the quantum behavior of the force of gravity. The classical description of gravity is explained in Einstein's General Theory of Relativity (through a malleable space-time manifold). Some theories of quantum gravity are used to explain a pre-Big Bang condition (prior to the advent of the space-time manifold described by the General Theory of Relativity). The two most popular theories are string theory and loop quantum gravity. This field of physics may remain quite hypothetical into the future, because its effects can only be observed near the Planck scale, which is far too small to be currently detected.

22 Inflation theory (first described by Alan Guth to resolve various problems in the standard Big Bang model) describes the extremely rapid exponential expansion of the early universe by a factor of at least 10^{78} in volume. The inflation epoch seems to have taken place in the first part of the electroweak era (when the universe was only 10^{-36} seconds to 10^{-33} seconds old). Inflation arises out of vacuum energy (dark

allow for the formation of four major speculative theories that might expand our view of physical reality far beyond our observable universe:

1. The *multiverse hypothesis*—inflationary theory allows for the possibility of a giant inflating universe that can produce a multiplicity of bubble universes indefinitely into the future. One such bubble universe would be our own.

2. The *bouncing universe* hypothesis—since the time of Albert Einstein, the conventional bouncing universe hypothesis took the general form of a cyclic universe that expanded and then contracted in a "big crunch," and then bounced and re-expanded repeatedly. The expansion from the Big Bang until today is theorized to be one such cycle—the last one amidst many others.

3. The *pre-Big Bang eternally static hypothesis*—quantum gravity allows for the possibility of

energy) which has the opposite effect of mass-energy on the space-time manifold. In the General Theory of Relativity, the density of mass-energy causes an increased curvature of the space-time manifold (giving rise to a force of attraction). However, the density of vacuum energy causes the space-time manifold to expand and stretch at an accelerated rate (causing a repulsive effect).

a pre-Big Bang era in which the universe was perfectly stable for a long period of time prior to the Big Bang.

4. The *higher dimensional space universe hypothesis*—string theory (particularly M Theory) allows for the possibility of universes to exist in higher dimensional space (consisting of, say, eleven dimensions), permitting unusual, complex expanding and bouncing universes. All of these hypotheses extend our view of physical reality beyond our observable universe, which may allow physical reality to exist prior to our 13.8-billion-year-old history (since the Big Bang)—and even eternally into the past. As I have noted, they are all completely hypothetical and lie beyond our current capacity to observe. They may, in principle, be unobservable. As we will see in sections III–V, every one of these scenarios very probably requires a *beginning in the finite past*, and for this reason brings physics to the threshold of metaphysics.

III.

Space-Time Geometry Proofs and the Beginning of Physical Reality

Lemaître's discovery of the expansion of space-time in the universe (as a whole) enabled physicists to formulate theorems (proofs) about the necessity of a beginning. All such proofs are based on various physical (observable) data that must all be true in order for the conclusion (about a beginning of the universe) to be true. They take the following general form: "If condition A, condition B, and condition C are true, then there must be a beginning of the universe (or the beginning of a multiverse or the beginning of physical reality itself)." The first space-time geometry proof (called a singularity theorem), proposed by Stephen Hawking and Roger Penrose between 1968 and 1970,[23] was based on five conditions. In 1980, Hawking declared, "a curvature singularity that will intersect every world line ... [makes] general relativity predict a beginning of time."[24] Twenty years after they formulated the proof, Alan Guth proposed an inflationary theory that appeared to violate the third condition of the Hawking-Penrose Proof ("the mass density and pressure of matter never become negative"). Inflation (presumably caused by dark energy) produces negative pressure (accelerating expansion), which violates the third condition of the proof. This was only a temporary setback for space-time geometry proofs of a beginning. In 1994, Arvind Borde and Alexander Vilenkin devised a proof for a singularity (and beginning of the universe) accounting for *inflationary* cosmology.[25] However, they found an exception to their proof in 1997 with regard to the weak energy condition. Even though this exception was highly unlikely in our universe, it re-opened the possibility of an eternal universe (in the past).[26] During the

23 Hawking and Penrose 1970, pp. 529–48.
24 Hawking 1980, p. 149.
25 Borde and Vilenkin 1994, pp. 3305–08.
26 Borde and Vilenkin 1997, p. 720.

same period, Alan Guth tried to show that all known mathematical configurations of inflationary-model cosmologies required a beginning.[27] Although Guth's study was comprehensive, it did not constitute a proof of a singularity in all inflationary cosmologies.

In 2003, all three joined together to formulate an elegant proof of a boundary to past time in all cosmologies where the average Hubble expansion is greater than zero. This proof is not dependent on the weak energy condition (which allowed for possible exceptions to the 1994 Borde-Vilenkin Proof). They formulated their findings as follows:

> Our argument shows that null and time-like geodesics are, in general, past-incomplete [requiring a boundary to past time]

27 Guth 1999, p. 13: "In my own opinion, it looks like eternally inflating models *necessarily* have a beginning. I believe this for two reasons. The first is the fact that, as hard as physicists have worked to try to construct an alternative, so far all the models that we construct have a beginning; they are eternal into the future, but not into the past. The second reason is that the technical assumption questioned in the 1997 Borde-Vilenkin paper does not seem important enough to me to change the *conclusion*."

in inflationary models, whether or not energy conditions hold, provided only that the averaged expansion condition $H_{av} > 0$ holds along these past-directed geodesics. This is a stronger conclusion than the one arrived at in previous work in that we have shown under reasonable assumptions that almost all causal geodesics, when extended to the past of an arbitrary point, reach the boundary of the inflating region of spacetime in a *finite* proper time.[28]

Remarkably, this proof (which will be explained in detail) has extensive general applicability—that is, to *any universe* with an average Hubble expansion greater than zero. In particular, it applies to the eternal inflation scenario. Vilenkin states it as follows:

We made no assumptions about the material content of the universe. We did not even assume that gravity is described by Einstein's equations. So, if Einstein's gravity requires some modification, our

28 Borde, Guth, and Vilenkin 2003, p. 3. Italics mine.

conclusion will still hold. The only assumption that we made was that the expansion rate of the universe never gets
below some nonzero value, no matter
how small. This assumption should certainly be satisfied in the inflating false
vacuum. The conclusion is that past-eter-
nal inflation without a beginning is impossible.[29]

The implications of Vilenkin's statement should
not be underestimated, for he is claiming that the
proof is valid almost *independently of the physics
of any universe* (except for the one condition that
the average expansion rate of the universe or multiverse be greater than zero). He is further claiming that such a universe without a beginning is
impossible. This proof is virtually universally applicable and very difficult to disprove (because it
has only one condition). Its importance merits further explanation (which can be done through logical steps with very little mathematical analysis).
The following five steps indicate the logical and
empirical validity of the proof.

29   Vilenkin 2006, p. 175.

The *first step* comes from Fr. Georges Lemaître in 1923—the farther a galaxy is from our galaxy, the greater will be its recessional velocity (its speed going away from the observer). Recall what was said about the universe expanding like a balloon—if space is stretching (growing like the elastic of our balloon), then the further a galaxy is from us (the observer), the greater its recessional velocity will be. Why? Because galaxies are not simply moving away from each other in fixed space; the space between the galaxies is actually stretching and growing (like the balloon). Thus, the more space there is between my galaxy and another galaxy, the more space there is to stretch and grow, and so we would expect that there would be more growing of space between our galaxy and a far distant galaxy than between our galaxy and a nearer one. This should increase the recessional velocity in proportion to a galaxy's distance from our galaxy. Hubble had a precise equation to calculate this: $v = H_0 D$ (where v is the recessional velocity of a distant galaxy, D is the proper distance of that galaxy from our galaxy, and H is the Hubble constant, which transforms proper distance into recessional velocity). Today the Hubble constant is thought to be 69.32 ± 0.80

(km/s)/Mpc (kilometer per second per mega-parsec).

We can illustrate this very simply with a rubber band. Take out a rubber band and put it on top of a ruler. Now draw a dot on the rubber band at point zero; another dot at one inch; and yet another dot at two inches. Now, take the rubber band and hold it with your left hand at point zero. With your right hand stretch the rubber band so that the dot that was at two inches is now at four inches. Evidently the dot that was at two inches from origin has expanded another two inches (to the four inch mark). But notice that the dot that was at the one inch mark has only moved to the *two-inch mark* (*an expansion of only one inch*). Thus, if space as a whole is growing like a balloon (or like our rubber band), the farther away a galaxy is from our galaxy (at point zero on the ruler) the more it expands per unit time. Since recessional velocity is "expansion per unit time" Lemaître proved his point—the farther away the galaxy is, the greater its recessional velocity will be—if space between the galaxies is expanding (instead of galaxies moving away from each other in fixed space).

The *second step*: We must now learn yet another concept—namely, relative velocity. This term refers to the velocity of a projectile (say, a rocket) approaching a galaxy that is moving away from it. Alexander Vilenkin gives the following example:

> Suppose, for example, the space traveler has just zoomed by the Earth at the speed of 100,000 kilometers per second and is now headed toward a distant galaxy, about a billion light-years away. That galaxy is moving away from us at 20,000 kilometers per second, so when the space traveler catches up with it, the observers there will see him moving at 80,000 kilometers per second [100,000 kps minus 20,000 kps].[30]

Now let us extend Vilenkin's example. Suppose that there are observers on a more distant galaxy—twice as far away as the first galaxy (two billion light years from here). Its recessional velocity should be approximately twice as much as the first galaxy's recessional velocity (approximately 40,000 kilometers per second away from us). The observers on that galaxy would see the

30   Vilenkin, 2006, p. 174.

rocket coming at 60,000 kps (100,000 kps minus 40,000 kps).

It is evident that relative velocity is inversely proportional to recessional velocities. So, the greater distance a galaxy is from us, the *greater* will be its recessional velocity; however, the *relative* velocity of a projectile approaching that more distant galaxy will be *smaller* than its relative velocity approaching a *nearer* galaxy. We can generalize by saying that the greater the distance of an object (such as a galaxy) is from a projectile (like a spaceship) moving toward it, the greater will be the recessional velocity of that object; however, the relative velocity of a projectile approaching it will be smaller (in inverse proportion to the recessional velocity).

The *third step*: There are two ways of having greater distance between our galaxy and other distant galaxies. The first way is the one described above (where galaxy #2 happens to be farther away than galaxy #1). The second way is by going into the *future*. Let us return to our example of the rubber band. If the universe is expanding like our rubber band, then every single moment our universe moves into the future, the recessional velocity of distant objects will get greater and greater. Remember our three dots: one at point zero, one at one inch, and one at two inches. When I pulled the third dot from two inches to four inches, the second dot only went from one inch to two inches. But now that the second dot is at two inches, it will do the same thing that the third dot did previously. It will now move from two inches to four inches in the same unit time. Thus, as our universe proceeds into the future, the recessional velocities of its galaxies will increase, because there is more space to expand (more rubber band to expand) between them.

The *fourth step*: let us now apply this insight about *recessional* velocities to *relative* velocities. Recall that recessional velocity and relative velocity are inversely proportional, so if recessional velocities are *increasing* into the future, relative velocities of approaching projectiles must be *decreasing* into the future. Since all galaxies are moving away from each other (because the universe's spatial manifold is expanding as a whole), all relative velocities of objects will have to move slower and slower into the future.

The *fifth step*: what is the consequence of step four? If the relative velocities of all objects must be getting slower and slower into the future, they must have been faster and faster in the past. Vilenkin puts it this way:

> If the velocity of the space traveler relative to the spectators gets smaller and smaller into the future, it follows that his velocity should get larger and larger as we follow his history into the past. In the limit, his velocity should get arbitrarily close to the speed of light.[31]

So what is the point? It is not possible to have a relative velocity greater than the speed of light in our universe. Thus, when all relative velocities were arbitrarily close to the speed of light, then the past time of our universe could not have gone back any further. It represents a *beginning* of the universe. Could this consequence of a beginning of the universe (in the Borde-Guth-Vilenkin Proof) be avoided if scientists discover a velocity higher than the speed of light in the future? No, because it does not matter what the upper limit to velocity is, it will always be reached in a finite proper time. The only thing that matters is that there *is* an upper limit to velocity in the universe (no matter

31   Vilenkin 2006, p. 175.

what it is). This upper limit would have to be reached in a finite proper time, and so the universe would have to have a beginning in *any* expansionary scenario—irrespective of the true upper limit to velocity in it.

Let us now suppose that scientists discover a tachyon (a particle that can travel faster than the speed of light) next year. Suppose further that this tachyon can travel at twice the speed of light (600,000 kps). Would this affect the BGV Proof? No, because the relative velocities of all projectiles would have been increasing in the same fashion (as I mentioned) throughout the universe's history, so at an earlier point in the universe's past, all relative velocities would have been 600,000 kps—which would again constitute a beginning (because the past time of the universe could not have existed before that point). We can postulate any finite velocity we want as the upper limit to velocity in our universe (or any other universe or a multiverse) and we can know with certainty that every projectile in that universe or multiverse would have been travelling at that relative velocity sometime in that universe's or multiverse's *finite* past. Every scenario *requires* a beginning.

Does *every* universe or multiverse have to have a *finite* maximum velocity? Yes, because if that finite upper limit did not exist, then physical energy could travel at an *infinite* velocity, in which case physical energy could be everywhere in the universe or multiverse simultaneously. This gives rise to two irresolvable problems—first, there would be a multiplication of the same physical energy at every space-time point in the universe. This multiplication of physical energy leads to a second problem—namely, that every space-time point would be simultaneously occupied by contradictory forms of energy (such as protons and electrons or matter and antimatter). The whole universe or multiverse would be filled with contradictions (an obviously impossible state of affairs). The avoidance of these problems requires a finite maximum velocity in every universe *and* multiverse (because every multiverse must be inflationary, and must therefore have an average expansion rate greater than zero). If all universes and multiverses must have a finite maximum velocity, and they also have an expansion rate greater than zero (the single condition of the BGV Proof), then they would also have to have a *beginning*.

There is one important nuance that should be clarified. The BGV Proof establishes a boundary. To the extent that classical gravity is operative near that boundary, the boundary is a singularity and therefore a beginning of time. However, if quantum gravity effects are important near that boundary (which would be the case in some scenarios), the boundary could merely be a gateway to another earlier region of space-time.[32] If the boundary represents only a transition to a new kind of physics, then the question arises as to whether that new physics is subject to a BGV boundary that is fundamental (such as a singularity or an absolute boundary to past time). This is where the extensive general applicability of the BGV Proof comes into play, for inasmuch as the Proof applies to *any* universe with an average Hubble expansion greater than zero (independent of the physics of that universe), the BGV Proof requires that a past-time boundary be present in any prior state of the universe that is expansive. Ultimately, an absolute boundary to all past expansive states will be reached (which would be a beginning of past time

---

32   See Borde, Guth, and Vilenkin 2003, p. 4. See also Craig and Sinclair 2009, p. 142 (n. 41).

in the universe). There is only one way to avoid this beginning—a prior state that is eternally static (which I will address later).

Borde, Guth, and Vilenkin respond to some scenarios of prior universal states arising out of quantum gravity and inflation. One such scenario is inspired by string theory:

> Our argument can be straightforwardly extended to cosmology in higher dimensions. For example, in [one model], brane worlds are created in collisions of bubbles nucleating in an inflating higher-dimensional bulk spacetime. Our analysis implies that the inflating bulk cannot be past-complete [that is, must have a boundary to past time]. We finally comment on the cyclic Universe model in which a bulk of four spatial dimensions is sandwiched between two three-dimensional branes. ... In some versions of the cyclic model the brane spacetimes are everywhere expanding, so our theorem immediately implies the existence of a past boundary at which boundary conditions must be imposed. In other versions, there are brief periods

of contraction, but the net result of each cycle is an expansion. ... Thus, as long as $H_{av} > 0$ for a null geodesic when averaged over one cycle, then $H_{av} > 0$ for any number of cycles, and our theorem would imply that the geodesic is incomplete [that is, must have a boundary to past time].[33]

Notice that the extensive general applicability of the BGV theorem allows it to establish a past-time boundary for quite diverse models where quantum gravity effects play important roles. Notice also that the BGV theorem applies to this hypothesis even though it has a contracting phase, because all that is required for the applicability of the BGV Proof is that the *average* Hubble expansion be greater than zero (no matter how small the positive non-zero average might be). Since this hypothetical condition must have an *average* Hubble expansion greater than zero (amidst its many expansions and contractions), it must have a boundary to its past time.

Does the BGV theorem apply also to Linde's eternal inflation scenario? According to Borde,

---

33 Borde, Guth, and Vilenkin 2003, p. 4.

Guth, and Vilenkin, it does. Linde originally suggested that each bubble universe begins with a singularity and further suggested that these regional singularities might mitigate the need for a singularity in the whole array of bubble universes.[34] Craig and Sinclair explain why this does not escape the Borde, Guth, and Vilenkin Proof:

> Andrei Linde has offered a critique, suggesting that BGV imply that all the individual parts of the universe have a beginning, but perhaps the WHOLE does not. This seems misconstrued, however, since BGV are *not* claiming that *each* past inextendible geodesic is related to a *regional* singularity. Rather, they claim that Linde's universe description contains an internal contradiction. As we look backward along the geodesic, it *must* extend to the infinite past if the universe is to be past eternal. But it does not (for the observer commoving with the expansion).[35]

34 See Linde 1998, p. 105.
35 Craig and Sinclair 2009, p. 142, n. 41.

The extensive general applicability of the BGV Proof (whose only condition is an average Hubble expansion greater than zero) makes possible exceptions fall within a very narrow range. A possible exception will have to postulate either (1) a universal model with an average Hubble expansion *less* than zero (that is, where average contraction is greater than expansion) or (2) a universal model where the average Hubble expansion is *equal* to zero (what is termed an "eternally static universe").

Since models postulating an average contraction greater than expansion have proven to be physically unrealistic, physicists have turned to the "eternally static hypothesis" to find a way out of the BGV Proof. Vilenkin and his graduate student, Audrey Mithani, have demonstrated significant physical problems with this hypothesis (particularly quantum instabilities which force the static state to break down in a finite time) in several important articles.[36] Additionally, the eternally static

---

36 An excellent summary of this work can be found in Vilenkin's lecture to the physics community at Cambridge University on the occasion of Stephen Hawking's 70th birthday. See http://www.newscientist.com/article/mg21328474.400-why-physicists-cant-avoid-a-creation-event.html.

hypothesis falls prey to an irresolvable logical contradiction. Craig and Sinclair sum up the fundamental (and seemingly insurmountable) problem as follows:

> [The asymptotically static hypothesis] has the dilemma that it must begin static and then transition to an expansion. Hence, the static phase is metastable, which implies that it is finite in lifetime. The universe begins to exist.[37]

Craig and Sinclair point to a fundamental contradiction in the eternally static hypothesis. In order for a universe to exist in a static state for an infinite time, it would have to be *perfectly* stable. However, for a universe to move from one state to another, say, from a quantum cosmological or string theory state (before the Big Bang) to a state described by the General Theory of Relativity (after the Big Bang), the quantum cosmological state would have to have been *metastable* (not perfectly stable) to accommodate the decay of the first state into the second one. This implies that the hypothesis is contradictory—because the

37   Craig and Sinclair 2009, p. 158.

quantum cosmological state would have to have been *both* "perfectly stable (to last for an eternity)" and "not perfectly stable (metastable in order to decay into an expansive state)" prior to the Big Bang.

In sum, there are three consequences of the Borde, Guth, and Vilenkin Proof:

1. It applies to all universes and multiverses (including bouncing universes in higher dimensions) that have an average rate of expansion greater than zero (no matter how small).

2. It does not matter what the physics of a given universe or multiverse might be; so long as the average Hubble expansion is greater than zero (because every universe or multiverse must have an upper limit to velocity).

3. Since there is only one condition for the proof to work and it functions independently of the physics of any given universe or multiverse, it will be very difficult to disprove.

At this point, it seems as if physics is coming very close to proving an absolute beginning of physical reality itself—whether physical reality is simply our universe, or perhaps a multiverse, or a universe in the higher dimensional space of string theory, or a static quantum cosmological state. If no physically realistic exception can be found to this proof (and to the problems of an eternally static universe), it would make an absolute beginning of physical reality quite probable. Vilenkin agrees with this assessment, and said in 2006:

> It is said that an argument is what convinces reasonable men and a proof [like the BGV Proof] is what it takes to convince even an unreasonable man. With the proof now in place, cosmologists can no longer hide behind the possibility of a past-eternal universe. There is no escape, they have to face the problem of a cosmic beginning.[38]

This takes us to the threshold of metaphysics. Before moving in that direction, we will want to first consider another vastly applicable datum that also indicates the likelihood of a beginning of physical reality—entropy.

38   Vilenkin 2006, p. 176.

IV.

Entropy and the Beginning of our Universe

Entropy is a technical concept that measures the degree of disorder or disorganization of a system. For purely probabilistic reasons, systems left to their own devices ("isolated systems") tend to evolve in a way that keeps the level of disorganization (entropy) constant or increases it. Almost never does the entropy of an isolated system decrease. Systems do not spontaneously get more organized. To make a system more organized takes something coming in from outside and expending energy (I can make the coffee in a cup hotter than its surroundings, for instance, by using a "heat pump"—the opposite of a refrigerator—to pump thermal energy from the cooler air into the hotter coffee. But that would require the expenditure of energy to run the heat pump).

The famous Second Law of Thermodynamics says that in isolated systems, entropy always increases or stays the same, and never goes down. That is why some processes are irreversible. If a process changes the entropy, then it can only go one way—the way that entropy (disorganization) increases. That is why dead bodies decompose, but do not recompose! Of course, these are, ultimately, probabilistic statements. Entropy can have random fluctuations downward, but these are usually very tiny decreases, and the larger the decrease in entropy, the more unlikely it is to happen. This is a universal phenomenon. It is why physicists regard "perpetual motion machines" as impossible. And here is the relevance to the question of whether the universe had a beginning. If the universe did not have a beginning, then it has been around for an infinite time. In a sense, the universe is then itself a "perpetual motion machine," a system that never "runs down" or "wears out," which is a violation of the Second Law of Thermodynamics.

This argument against an infinite universe can be broken down into five steps:

1. For a physical system to do work, it needs to have order (disequilibrium)[39] within it. Variations of temperature (or other factors such as pressure or molecular distribution) within a system enable it to do physically useful work.

2. Every time a physical system does work it loses a small amount of its order (disequilibrium), which means that it is not capable of doing as much work as it could in its previous state. This movement from order to disorder is called "entropy."

3. For statistical reasons alone, entropy (the movement from order to disorder) is irreversible in the long term (though there may be random fluctuations toward lower entropy which do not and cannot last long).

---

39 "Order" generally refers to disequilibrium (such as variation in temperature, or differentiation of molecular distribution, or differentiation of pressure within a physical system). Since all thermodynamic systems tend toward equilibrium (the same temperature or distribution of molecules or pressure within a system), it follows that equilibrium is the most probable state of a system—and is considered the most disordered. In contrast to this, the more disequilibrium there is in a system, the more it is said to be ordered or organized (which is a more improbable state).

4. If the universe is an isolated[40] physical system (the assumption of the standard Big Bang model), then the universe could not have existed for an infinite amount of time, because if it did, it would be at a state of maximum entropy (maximum equilibrium) today (for the reasons stated in 1–3 above). It would be a dead universe incapable of any work.

5. But the universe is not at maximum entropy (maximum equilibrium); there are hot stars and cold space, galactic clusters and empty space, and physical systems are continuously working—stars burning, planets forming, and physicists thinking about it. Therefore, the universe has not existed for an infinite amount of time (and therefore has a beginning).

The evidence of entropy has one important quality in common with that of the Borde-Guth-Vilenkin Proof, namely, its vast applicability (seemingly to every physical system). I stated earlier that the Second Law of Thermodynamics

---

40 "Isolated" here refers to a system acting on its own. There is no engine or heating element outside the physical system that can introduce additional order (disequilibrium) within the system.

(entropy) is valid for statistical (mathematical) reasons alone. Therefore, it is applicable to a multiplicity of physical scenarios—and is theoretically applicable to virtually every physical system. Why? Because disequilibrium (order) is so much more improbable than equilibrium (disorder) and every physical system will always follow a line toward greatest probability—that is, toward disorder. Einstein was so certain of this that he declared:

> A theory is the more impressive the greater the simplicity of its premises is, the more different kinds of things it relates, and the more extended is its area of applicability. ... [Entropy] is the only physical theory of a universal content concerning which I am convinced that within the framework of the applicability of its basic concepts, it will never be overthrown.[41]

There has been no shortage of attempts to elude this consequence of the Second Law of Thermodynamics (entropy). Several physicists have

41   Quoted in Holton and Elkana 1997, p. 227.

suggested that entropy might be lowered in a universal collapse ("a big crunch") or in a bouncing universe scenario. Both of these suggestions have been virtually ruled out by the research of Roger Penrose,[42] Sean Carroll,[43] and Thomas Banks and

42 As I will discuss (section V), Roger Penrose shows the virtual impossibility of low entropy at a bounce, because the odds against it are $10^{10^{123}}$ to 1 against its occurrence (the odds of a monkey typing Macbeth by random tapping of the keys in one try—this is a virtual impossibility). See Penrose 1989, pp. 343–44.

43 According to Sean Carroll, a well-known cosmologist, the low entropy of our universe at the Big Bang invalidates an eternal bouncing universe hypothesis; it even makes a single bounce to be exceedingly improbable: "Bojowald uses some ideas from Loop Quantum Gravity to try to resolve the initial singularity and follow the quantum state of the universe past the [Big] Bang back into a pre-existing universe. If you try to invent a cosmology in which you straightforwardly replace the singular Big Bang by a smooth Big Bounce continuation into a previous space-time, you have one of two choices: either the entropy continues to decrease as we travel backwards in time through the Bang, or it changes direction and begins to increase. Sadly, neither makes any sense. If you are imagining that the arrow of time is continuous as you travel back through the Bounce, then you are positing a very strange universe indeed on the

Willy Fischler.[44] They also show that entropy makes virtually every form of the bouncing uni-

other side. It is one in which the infinite past has an extremely tiny entropy, which increases only very slightly as the universe collapses, so that it can come out the other side in our observed low-entropy state. That requires the state at t = minus infinity state of the universe to be infinitely finely tuned, for no apparent reason (the same holds true for the Steinhardt-Turok cyclic universe). On the other hand, if you imagine that the arrow of time reverses direction at the Bounce, you've moved your extremely-finely-tuned-for-no-good-reason condition to the Bounce itself. In models where the Big Bang is really the beginning of the universe, one could in principle imagine that some unknown law of physics makes the boundary conditions there very special, and explains the low entropy (a possibility that Roger Penrose, for example, has taken seriously). But if it is not a boundary, why are the conditions there [at the Bounce] so special?" (Carroll 2007, p. 1).

44 Banks and Fischler believe that a universal collapse will lead to a "black crunch" (maximum entropy) from which a low entropy bounce would be virtually impossible ($10^{10^{123}}$ to 1 against, according to Roger Penrose—see section V). In fact, things are probably even worse for models in which the Big Bang was a bounce preceded by a phase in which the universe was collapsing. It has been argued by the particle physicists, Banks and Fischler, that during such a collapse

verse hypothesis untenable.[45] Although physicists are still hypothesizing new scenarios to elude a beginning of the universe from entropy, they are be-

> the rapidly changing space-time would have excited and amplified random "quantum fluctuations" in such a way that entropy would have been driven to very *large* values, rather than small ones. This makes it even more difficult to account for the fantastically low entropy just after the Big Bang. In Banks's words, "I have a problem with ALL cyclic cosmologies …. The collapsing phase of these models always has a time-dependent Hamiltonian for the quantum field fluctuations around the classical background. Furthermore the classical backgrounds are becoming singular. This means that the field theories will be excited to higher and higher energy states …. High energy states in field theory have the ergodic property—they thermalize rapidly, in the sense that the system explores all of its states. Willy Fischler and I proposed that in this situation you would again tend to maximize the entropy. We called this a black crunch and suggested the equation of state of matter would again tend toward $p = \rho$. It seems silly to imagine that, even if this is followed by a re-expansion, that one would start that expansion with a low entropy initial state, or that one had any control over the initial state at all" (Banks 2007, from a private communication to James Sinclair, October 12, 2007, in Craig and Sinclair 2009, p. 156).

45   See the previous three footnotes.

coming more and more fantastic and further and further removed from the domain of observable evidence and the discipline of physics.

V.

From Physics to Metaphysics

The discussion in the two foregoing sections shows a preponderance of cosmological evidence favoring a beginning of the universe (prior to which there was no physical reality). This beginning of physical reality marks the point at which our universe (and even a hypothetical multiverse or a universe in the higher dimensional space of string theory) came into existence. Recall (from section II) that quantum gravity and inflation theory allowed for four major hypothetical extensions of physical reality beyond our observable universe and prior to our Big Bang: the multiverse hypothesis, the bouncing universe hypothesis, the eternally static universe hypothesis, and the higher dimensional space hypothesis. The foregoing analysis shows the probability that all four of these hypothetical models have a beginning for the following reasons:

1. Every multiverse hypothesis must be inflationary, subjecting it to the Borde-Guth-Vilenkin Proof, which entails a beginning in the finite past.

2. Bouncing universe hypotheses fall prey to four major problems: they are subject to (a) the Borde-Guth-Vilenkin Proof (because their average Hubble expansion is greater than zero), (b) Carroll's requirement of "infinite fine-tuning for no apparent reason" in eternally bouncing universes (making them virtually impossible), (c) Banks's and Fischler's prediction that a single collapse will lead to a dark dead universe (maximum entropy), and (d) the probable flat geometry and preponderance of dark energy in our universe disallows the cessation of expansion into the future.

3. The eternally static hypothesis falls prey to quantum instabilities according to Vilenkin and Mithani. It also appears to be intrinsically contradictory (perfectly stable and not perfectly stable prior to the Big Bang).

4. The expanding and bouncing forms of the higher dimensional space hypothesis are subject to the Borde-Guth-Vilenkin Proof, which entails a beginning in a finite past time. There are

currently no truly satisfactory alternatives to this evidence for a beginning.[46] Is this evidence sufficient to show a beginning of *physical reality itself*?

If a beginning of physical reality is a point at which everything physical (including mass-energy, space and time, and physical laws and constants) came into existence, then *prior* to this beginning, all aspects of physical reality would have been *nothing*. It seems likely that this is the case, because quantum gravity, the General Theory of Relativity, and field theory all suggest that everything physical is interrelated[47]—if one aspect

46 Since the Borde-Guth-Vilenkin theorem rules out all expanding universes (or multiverses), and the entropy evidence rules out an eternal universe and all bouncing universes, and the static universe hypothesis is intrinsically contradictory and highly improbable in light of quantum instabilities, the only recourse left seems to be that of postulating "backward time" prior to the Big Bang (see Aguirre and Gratton 2002). Physicists have declared this hypothesis to be physically unrealistic because it enables physically unrealistic phenomena to occur—such as the sound of the clap coming before the clap.

47 Some may think that space and time are not relevant in quantum gravity (for example, String Theory or Loop Quantum Gravity), but in fact, they are. String Theory and Loop Quantum Gravity presume conti-

exists, then they all exist, and vice-versa. This means that prior to the beginning, physical reality was most likely nothing—physical space and time, physical mass and energy, and the laws and constants—every aspect of physical reality. This encounter with "nothing" brings us into the domain of metaphysics, which many physicists have unwittingly entered because of the strong evidence for a beginning of physical reality. Stephen Hawking has recently claimed that spontaneous creation can occur from nothing, because of the law of gravitation and M Theory.[48] Alexander Vilenkin has a more developed view of Hawking's central point—that the universe tunneled from nothing (which turns out to be irresolvably problematic). He seems to recognize problems in this hypothesis, and backs into a position of "closet theism." William Lane Craig provides a summary and

nuity, dimensionality, and temporal differentiation (space and time), but they are differently configured than in the General Theory of Relativity.

48 Hawking and Mlodinow 2010, p. 180: "Because there is a law such as gravity, the Universe can and will create itself from nothing .... Spontaneous creation is the reason there is something rather than nothing, why the Universe exists, why we exist."

incisive critique of Vilenkin's argument in his re-view of Vilenkin's 2006 book, *Many Worlds in One: The Search for Other Universes:*

> [Vilenkin] invites us to envision a small, closed, spherical universe filled with a false vacuum and containing some ordinary matter. If the radius of such a universe is small, classical physics predicts that it will collapse to a point; but quantum physics permits it to "tunnel" into a state of inflation .... If we allow the radius to shrink all the way to zero, there still remains some positive probability of the universe's tunneling to inflation. Now Vilenkin equates the initial state of the universe explanatorily prior to tunneling with nothingness: "what I had was a mathematical description of a universe tunneling from zero size—from nothing!—to a finite radius and beginning to inflate" (180). This equivalence is patently mistaken. As Vilenkin's diagram on the same page illustrates, the quantum tunneling is at every point a function from something to something. For

quantum tunneling to be truly from nothing, the function would have to have a single term, the posterior term. Another way of seeing the point is to reflect on the fact that to have no radius (as is the case with nothingness) is not to have a radius whose measure is zero.

Vilenkin himself seems to realize that he has not really described the tunneling of the universe from literally nothing, for he allows, "And yet, the state of 'nothing' cannot be identified with *absolute nothingness*. The tunneling is described by the laws of quantum mechanics, and thus 'nothing' should be subjected to these laws" (181). It follows that the universe described by those laws is not nothing. Unfortunately, Vilenkin draws the mistaken inference that "The laws of physics must have existed, even though there was no universe" (181). Even if one takes a Platonistic view of the laws of nature, they are at most either mathematical objects or propositions, abstract entities that have no effect on anything. (Intriguingly, Vilenkin entertains a

conceptualist view according to which
the laws exist in a mind which predates
the universe [205], the closest Vilenkin
comes to theism.)[49]

As Craig shows, Vilenkin implicitly recognizes his
equivocation concerning the term "nothing" and
this ultimately requires him to postulate the existence of physical laws independent of the universe. He also seems to recognize that these laws
imply a transphysical mind or mentative state,
which, as Craig notes, puts him in the camp of
implicit theism. In my view, Vilenkin's metaphysical foray is much more sophisticated than that
of Hawking and Mlodinow, because they do not
admit their equivocation about "nothing" and do
not acknowledge that their transphysical laws
(the law of gravitation and M Theory) entail a
transphysical mind or mentative state.[50] It seems

49 Craig 2009, p. 237.
50 At one time, Hawking did admit to the need for a
    transcendent cause beyond the laws of physics: "If we
    discover a complete theory, it would be the ultimate
    triumph of human reason—for then we should know
    the mind of God .... Even if there is only one possible
    unified theory, it is just a set of rules and equations.
    What is it that breathes fire into the equations and

that any attempt to hypothesize something coming from nothing will result in a host of problems—such as "sneaking" something into nothing, equivocating on the term "nothing," and/or postulating an unacknowledged transphysical mentative state which allows laws (without physical reality) to generate the whole of physical reality. If we are to avoid these confusions, we should follow the example of Parmenides, and allow "nothing" to be nothing (the complete absence of reality). This means not putting any content into "nothing" such as continuity, dimensionality, or orientability (as might be found in a spatial manifold) or confusing "nothing" with physical laws without a physical universe (entailing an unacknowledged transphysical mind or mentative state). Anything else argues the most fundamental of contradictions. We can know something else about nothing — namely, that it can only do nothing. As metaphysicians since the time of Parmenides have recognized, "From nothing, only nothing can come."

We may now proceed to our conclusion—

makes a universe for them to describe?" (Hawking 1988, p. 174).

combining a first premise from physics and a second premise from metaphysics:

> There is a likelihood of a beginning of physical reality (prior to which physical reality was literally nothing).
>
> From nothing, only nothing comes (*a priori* true).
>
> Therefore, it is likely that the universe came from *something* which is *not* physical reality (that is, beyond physical reality). This is commonly referred to as a "transcendent cause of the universe" (or "a transcendent cause of physical reality")—in short, "a Creator."

VI.

Fine-Tuning "for Life" at the Big Bang: Implications of Supernatural Intelligence

There are several conditions of our universe necessary for the emergence of any complex life form. Many of these conditions are so exceedingly improbable that it is not reasonable to expect that they could have occurred by pure chance. For this reason many physicists attribute their occurrence to supernatural design. Some other physicists prefer to believe instead in trillions upon trillions of "other universes" (in a multiverse which is unobserved and likely unobservable). Before discussing which explanation is more probative, we need to explore some specific instances of this highly improbable fine-tuning. We may break the discussion into two parts: (A) the exceedingly high improbability of our low entropy universe, and (B) the exceedingly high improbability of the anthropic values of our universe's constants. We will discuss each in turn.

A. The high improbability of a pure chance occurrence of our low-entropy universe

A low-entropy universe is necessary for the emergence, evolution, and complexification of life forms (because a high entropy universe would be too run-down to allow for such development). Roger Penrose has calculated the exceedingly small probability of a pure chance occurrence of our low-entropy universe at the Big Bang as $10^{10^{123}}$ to one against. How can we understand this number? It is like a ten raised to an exponent of 100,000,000,000,000,000,000,000,000,000,

000,000,000,000,000,000,000,000,000,000,000,
000,000,000,000,000,000,000,000,000,000,000,
000,000,000,000,000,000,000,000,000. This
number is so large that if every zero were 10-point
type, our solar system would not be able to hold it!
This is about the same odds as a monkey typing
Shakespeare's *Macbeth* by random tapping of the
keys in a single attempt (virtually impossible). Currently, there is no natural explanation for the occurrence of this number, and if none is found, then we
are left with the words of Roger Penrose himself:

> In order to produce a universe resem-
> bling the one in which we live, the *Cre-*
> *ator* would have to aim for an absurdly
> tiny volume of the phase space of possi-
> ble universes—about $1/10^{10^{123}}$ of the en-
> tire volume, for the situation under
> consideration.[51]

What Penrose is saying here is that this occurrence
cannot be explained by a random (pure chance) occurrence. Therefore, one will have to make recourse
either to a multiverse (composed of bubble universes,

51   Penrose 1989, p. 343.

each having different values of constants) or as Penrose implies, a Creator (with a super-intellect).

B. The high improbability of other anthropic conditions (based on universal constants)

A universal constant is a number that controls the equations of physics, and the equations of physics, in turn, describe the laws of nature. Therefore, these numbers control the laws of nature (and whether these laws of nature will be hospitable or hostile to any life form). Some examples of constants are: the speed of light constant (c = 300,000 km per second), Planck's constant ($\hbar = 6.6 \times 10^{-34}$ joule seconds), the gravitational attraction constant (G = 6.67×10^{-11}), the strong nuclear force coupling constant (g_s = 15), the weak force constant ($g_w = 1.43 \times 10^{-62}$), the rest mass of the proton (m_p = 1.67×10^{-27} kg), the rest mass of an electron (m_e = 9.11×10^{-31} kg), and the charge of an electron proton (e = 1.6×10^{-19} coulombs). There are several other constants, but the above constants are sufficient to show the fine-tuning of our universe.

Before proceeding to some examples, it should be noted that the constants could have been virtually any value (higher or lower) within a very broad range at the Big Bang. However, the range of values of the constants that will allow for the development of a life form is exceedingly small (given the essential laws of physics and the mass of the universe). This means that any life form is exceedingly exceedingly improbable.

Notice also that the Big Bang is thought to be a boundary condition to natural causation in our universe, because what preceded the Big Bang was not the universe described by the General Theory of Relativity (with a space-time manifold), but rather what might be called "a quantum cosmological universe" (described perhaps by string theory or by loop quantum gravity). This hypothetical pre-Big Bang configuration would be causally *distinct* from the universe described by the General Theory of Relativity (after the Big Bang). This makes it very difficult to appeal to some kind of prior *natural* causation to account for the values of our constants and the low entropy of our universe at the Big Bang. It virtually forces physicists to answer the question with either a multiverse or supernatural design (explained below). We may now proceed to some examples of how the constants' values are fine-tuned for life.

If the gravitational constant (G) or weak force constant (g_w) varied from their values by an exceedingly small fraction (higher *or* lower) —one part in 10^{50} (that is, .000000000000 000000000000000000000000000000000001) —then the universe would have either suffered a catastrophic collapse or exploded throughout its expansion, both of which options would have prevented the emergence and development of *any* life form. Paul Davies describes it as follows:

> If G, or g_w, differed from their actual values by even *one part in 10^{50}*, the precise balance against Λ_{bare} would be upset, and the structure of the uni verse would be drastically altered.[52] [I]f Λ were several orders of magnitude greater, the expansion of the universe would be explosive, and it is doubtful if galaxies could ever have formed against such a disruptive force. If Λ were negative, the explosion would be

52 Davies 1982, p. 107. Italics mine.

replaced by a catastrophic collapse of the universe. It is truly extraordinary that such dramatic effects would result from changes in the strength of either gravity, or the weak force, of less than one part in 10^{40}.[53]

This cannot be reasonably explained by a single random occurrence.

If the strong nuclear force constant were higher than its value (15) by only 2%, there would be no hydrogen in the universe (and therefore no nuclear fuel or water, prohibiting the development of a life form). If, on the other hand, the strong nuclear force constant had been 2% lower than its value then no element heavier than hydrogen could have emerged in the universe (helium, carbon, etc.). This would have prevented the development of a life form from the periodic table (specifically carbon-based life forms). Walter Bradley sums up Brandon Carter's research on this topic by noting that

> Brandon Carter in 1970 showed that a 2 percent reduction in the strong force and its associated constant would preclude

53   Davies 1982, p. 108.

the formation of nuclei with larger numbers of protons, making the formation of elements heavier than hydrogen impossible. On the other hand, if the strong force and associated constant were just 2 percent greater than it is, then all hydrogen would be converted to helium and heavier elements from the beginning, leaving the universe no water and no long-term fuel for the stars. The absolute value of the strong force constant, and more importantly, its value relative to the electromagnetic force constant is not "prescribed" by any physical theories, but it is certainly a critical *requirement* for a universe suitable for life.[54]

This "anthropic coincidence" also seems to lie beyond the boundaries of pure chance.

If the gravitational constant, electromagnetism, or the "proton mass relative to the electron mass" varied from their values by only a tiny fraction (higher *or* lower), then all stars would be either blue giants or red dwarfs. These kinds of stars

54 Bradley 1998, p. 39. Italics mine. See also Breuer 1991, p. 183.

would not emit the proper kind of heat and light for a long enough period to allow for the emergence, development, and complexification of life forms. Paul Davies outlines this coincidence as follows:

> What is remarkable is that this typical mass M_* just happens to lie in the narrow range between the blue giants and red dwarfs. This circumstance is in turn a consequence of an apparently accidental relation between the relative strengths of gravity and electromagnetism, as will be shown.[55]
>
> This remarkable relation compares the strength of gravity (on the left) with the strength of electromagnetism, and the ratio of electron to proton mass. ... Putting in the numbers, one obtains 5.9×10^{-39} for the left hand side, and 2.0×10^{-39} for the right hand side. Nature has evidently picked the values of the fundamental constants in such a way that typical stars lie very close indeed to the

55 Davies 1982, pp. 71–2.

boundary of convective instability. The fact that the two sides of the inequality (3.9) are such enormous numbers, and yet lie so close to one another [namely, 10^{-39}], *is truly astonishing.* If gravity were *very* slightly weaker, or electromagnetism *very* slightly stronger (or the electron slightly less massive relative to the proton), all stars would be *red dwarfs.* A correspondingly tiny change the other way, and they would all be *blue giants.*[56]

Again, this "anthropic coincidence" is inexplicable by a single random occurrence.

Fred Hoyle and William Fowler discovered the exceedingly high improbability of oxygen, carbon, helium, and beryllium having the precise values to allow for both carbon abundance and carbon bonding (necessary for life). This "anthropic coincidence" was so striking that it caused Hoyle to abandon his former atheism and declare, "A common sense interpretation of the facts suggests that a superintellect has monkeyed with physics, as well as with chemistry and biology,

---

56   Davies 1982, p. 73. Italics mine.

and that there are no blind forces worth speaking about in nature. The numbers one calculates from the facts seem to me so overwhelming as to put this conclusion almost beyond question."[57]

The vast majority of physicists do not attribute these four and other anthropic coincidences (or the low entropy of the universe) at the Big Bang to random occurrence. Neither do they appeal to a prior natural cause (since the low entropy and constant values occur at the Big Bang). This virtually forces physicists to select one of two transuniversal explanations: a multiverse in which every bubble universe has its own set of constant values, ultimately allowing trillions upon trillions upon trillions of bubble universes with different values of constants to naturalistically produce one highly improbable anthropic universe like our own; or, a supernatural design in which a highly intelligent transphysical Creator selects the values of the constants and produces the low entropy of the universe at the Big Bang (similar to Sir Fred Hoyle's "superintellect").

Is the multiverse hypothesis more reasonable and responsible than supernatural intelligence?

57 Hoyle 1981, pp. 8–12.

A combination of four factors implies that it is not. First, the other universes (and the multiverse itself) are, in principle, unobservable (beyond our event horizon). Second, the multiverse hypothesis violates the principle of parsimony (Ockham's Razor)—the explanation with the least number of assumptions, conditions, and requirements is to be preferred (because nature favors elegance over needless complexity). Paul Davies notes:

> Another weakness of the anthropic argument is that it seems the very antithesis of Occam's razor, according to which the most plausible of a possible set of explanations is that which contains the simplest ideas and least number of assumptions. To invoke an infinity of other universes just to explain one is surely carrying excess baggage to cosmic extremes, …. It is hard to see how such a purely theoretical construct can ever be used as an *explanation*, in the scientific sense, of a feature of nature. Of course, one might find it easier to believe in an infinite array of universes than in an in-

finite Deity, but such a belief must rest on faith rather than observation.[58]

Although the first two reasons do not invalidate the multiverse hypothesis, they indicate problems for using it as a scientific or naturalistic explanation. The third factor concerns the requirement that every multiverse have a beginning because every multiverse must be inflationary (have an expansion rate greater than zero), making it subject to the Borde-Guth-Vilenkin Proof. This means that no plausible multiverse could produce an unlimited number of bubble universes. Again, this factor alone does not invalidate the multiverse as a possible explanation for our highly improbable anthropic universe, because a multiverse could theoretically produce $10^{10^{123}}$ (or more!) bubble universes. However, when the above three factors are combined with the fourth, it raises serious doubts about the adequacy of the multiverse as an explanation of anthropic coincidences. The fourth factor concerns fine-tuning in the multiverse itself. Currently, all known multiverse theories have significant fine-tuning requirements. Linde's

58 Davies 1983, pp. 173–4.

Chaotic Inflationary Multiverse cannot randomly cough out bubble universes because they would collide and make the bubble universes inhospitable to life; the bubble universes must be spaced out in a slow roll which requires considerable fine-tuning in the multiverses' initial parameters.[59] Similarly, Susskind's String Theory Landscape requires considerable meta-level fine-tuning to explain its "anthropic tendencies."[60] In view of the above four factors, many physicists consider the supernatural design hypothesis to be just as reasonable and responsible (if not more reasonable and responsible) than the multiverse hypothesis for explaining the occurrence of our highly improbable anthropic universe.

Some physicists and philosophers have tried to cast doubt on the supernatural design hypothesis by appealing to a seemingly logical problem—namely that a designer would seem to be more improbable than anything it could design. Richard Dawkins is the best known advocate of this position, and we will need to respond to him if the supernatural intelligence hypothesis is to be plau-

59 See Alabidi and Lyth 2006.
60 See Gordon 2010, pp. 100–02.

sible and verifiable. As we shall see, Dawkins's contention is metaphysical (philosophical), and so we will have to make recourse to philosophical method to respond to him.

VII.

Richard Dawkins's Objection and a Thomistic[61] Metaphysical Response

Richard Dawkins has proffered a well-known objection to the fine-tuning argument for supernatural

61 I have deliberately not used technical terms from the works of Thomas Aquinas in my proof of the "unique, unrestricted, uncaused cause of all else that is, which is absolutely simple and an unrestricted act of thinking," because I wanted to make the proof as accessible as possible to the widest possible audience. However, any Thomist will recognize that I have borrowed virtually every part of the proof from the metaphysics of St. Thomas Aquinas, and that I owe him a complete debt of gratitude. Therefore, I provided texts from St. Thomas's works in footnotes in the ti-

intelligence (just given). Perhaps the most incisive way of responding to this objection is the metaphysical proof of God originally set out in Aquinas's early tractate *De ente et essentia* (and further elaborated in the *Summa contra gentiles* and the *Summa theologica*). The response will be given in four subsections:

A. Richard Dawkins's Objection;
B. An Eight-Step Thomistic Proof of God;
C. A Response to Richard Dawkins;
D. A Metaphysics of Restricted Being.

A. Richard Dawkins's Objection

Richard Dawkins's core argument in *The God Delusion* may be summarized as follows:

> A designer must always be more complex than what it designs.
> Whatever is more complex is more improbable.

tles of each step of the proof. I hope this will open up the metaphysics of Thomas Aquinas to those who are currently engaged in the debate with Richard Dawkins (and others like him) who apparently do not understand what he was attempting to demonstrate.

> Therefore, a designer must be more improbable than what it designs.[62]

There can be little doubt that Dawkins's second premise ("whatever is more complex is more improbable") is true, because the more complex a reality is, the more parts there are to order or organize. Since order or organization is more improbable than disorder, it follows that the more parts there are to order, the more improbable the ordering will be.

However, Dawkins's first premise is highly contestable and quite frankly, it ignores 2,400 years of philosophical history[63] going back to Plato and Aristotle, then proceeding to Augustine and Aquinas and then to contemporary philosophers such as Étienne Gilson, Josef Pieper, Bernard Lonergan, Karl Rahner, and all their followers.

---

62 Dawkins 2008, pp. 157–8.
63 Dawkins makes a perfunctory criticism of Aquinas's proofs for the existence of God (Dawkins 2008, pp. 100–03), but regrettably does not understand these proofs in any meaningful way. If he had, he would not have constructed a virtual "straw man" version of them, while missing the solution to one of the greatest metaphysical problems—the connection between an uncaused cause, absolute simplicity, and the nature of mentation (thinking).

These philosophers maintain that an uncaused cause (a creator and designer) would have to be absolutely simple (a complete absence of complexity) instead of more complex. Ironically, this means by Dawkins's second premise ("whatever is more complex is more improbable") that an absolutely simple Creator or designer would have to be the most probable reality of all.

B. An Eight-Step Thomistic Metaphysical Proof of God

The following eight-step argument represents a basic outline of what Dawkins failed to understand (and present) in his survey of philosophical arguments for God and his dismissal of Thomas Aquinas's proofs[64] in *The God Delusion*.

Definitions

"Caused Cause": A caused cause is a reality that does not exist through itself—it is depend-

---

64   Dawkins 2008, chap. 3, esp. pp. 100–103.

ent on causation for existence and must therefore await causation in order to exist. Without causation, it is merely hypothetical, and literally nothing. Causes include constituent parts or conditions for something to exist; for example, cells are composed of proteins and amino acids, which in turn are composed of molecules, which in turn are composed of atoms, etc. This would also include necessary structures and organizing components of those constituent parts, such as the particular structures of proteins, amino acids, molecules, etc. Without these constituent parts, conditions, and organizing structures, the cell would not exist. These causes are called "formal and material causes." Additionally, any element "outside" of a reality necessary for its existence would also be a cause—such as light, water, and nutriment for a cell's metabolism. These are called "efficient causes."

"*Uncaused Cause*": A reality that does not require any cause to exist. It exists purely through itself without any conditions whatsoever. As will be seen, it must be a pure act of existing through itself.

Step 1: There must exist at least one uncaused cause[65]

Recall that a caused cause must await causation in order to exist. Now, if the whole of reality were composed only of caused causes (realities that must await causation to exist), then the whole of reality would be awaiting causation to exist. If there were no uncaused cause in the whole of reality, then there would be no existing cause of the caused cause's existence—and therefore, the whole of reality would be literally nothing—awaiting causation to exist. Therefore, there must be at least one reality that does not have to await causation to exist (which exists through itself alone) and causes the existence of realities awaiting that causation. Without this

---

65 Aristotle first formulated this proof (as an "Unmoved Mover" Proof) in Book 8 of the *Physics* and Book 12 of the *Metaphysics*. The proof was later expanded to the "Uncaused Cause" Proof by Thomas Aquinas, and there are many versions of it today (see for example, chap. 19 of Bernard Lonergan's *Insight: A Study of Human Understanding*). St. Thomas Aquinas discusses this in a variety of different places, but for the most-well known see *Summa theologica* I, qu. 2, art. 3.

uncaused cause, the whole of reality would be literally nothing.

Further explanation: It does not matter whether one postulates an *infinite* number of caused causes (realities awaiting causation to exist), because an infinite number of postulated realities awaiting causation to exist (without an existing cause) is collectively still awaiting causation to exist—it is literally an infinite amount of nothing, and an infinite amount of nothing is still nothing.

Step 2: An uncaused cause must be the pure act of existing through itself[66]

As shown in step 1, there must be at least one uncaused cause—at least one reality which does not await causation to exist. What is a reality that does not await causation to exist? It must be one that exists through itself alone (for if it did not, it would need and await causation to exist). Thus, the uncaused cause must have the power to exist through itself, and more than this, that power

---

66 This insight is perhaps the crowning achievement of St. Thomas Aquinas's metaphysics. One excellent articulation of it may be found in *Summa contra gentiles*, Book 1, chap. 16, par. 3.

must be active—it must be an acting power to exist through itself alone, and so Thomas Aquinas called it "the act of existing through itself." Inasmuch as an uncaused cause would have to be an act of existing through itself *alone*, it must also be a *pure* act of existing through itself. The word "pure" here is important because there cannot be *anything* in the "act of existing through itself" which is different from it. If there were anything other than the "act of existing through itself" in it, that part or dimension of it would *not* exist through itself, and would therefore have to be caused. Since an uncaused cause cannot have a part or dimension which needs to be caused, it must be a *pure* "act of existing through itself."

Step 3: A pure act of existing through itself must be unrestricted[67]

Whatever restricts a pure act of existing through itself would have to be *different* from it because

---

67 This crucial insight is first developed by St. Thomas in his early metaphysical work *De ente et essentia* (*On Being and Essence*), particularly chaps. 4 and 5. For Thomas's view of "infinity" (in the sense of "unrestricted existence"), see *Summa contra gentiles*, Book 1, chap. 43, par. 1 and 3.

"what restricts" is different from what is restricted. This can be understood in four substeps: There are three main ways in which realities are restricted:

1. spatial restrictions—which limit a reality to existence at particular places (through a contemporaneous manifold which is divisible into "here and there");

2. temporal restrictions—which limit a reality to existing at particular times (through a non-contemporaneous manifold which is divisible into earlier and later);

3. restrictions as to a particular *way* of existing (such as the way of existing like an electron or a proton).

All of these restrictions must be *different* from an act of existing through itself:

1. A spatial restriction (which restricts existence to a particular place) must be different from an act of existing through itself because existence is not limited by nature to any particular place, and it does not by nature have to be in space (conditioned by a spatial manifold).

2. A temporal restriction (which restricts existence to a particular time) would have to be different from an act of existing through itself

because existence is not limited by nature to any particular time, and it does not by nature have to be in time (conditioned by a temporal manifold).

3. A restricted way of existing (such as the way of existing like a proton or an electron) would have to be different from an act of existing through itself because existence is not limited by nature to existing in the way of an electron, a proton, or *any* other restricted way of existing.

If every restriction must be different from the act of existing through itself, then these restrictions cannot exist through themselves, meaning that they must be caused (that is, they must all be caused through the agency of something else). If an uncaused cause is *completely* uncaused, then it must *completely* exist through itself. This means there can be nothing in it that is *caused* (that does not exist through itself). Now, if every restriction must be caused (because it is different from an act of existing through itself), then an uncaused cause must be unrestricted.

Therefore, a pure uncaused cause is "an unrestricted act of existing through itself." It cannot have any restrictions with respect to space, time, or restricted way of existing.

One last clarification. The term "unrestricted" refers to the absence of restriction within the act of existing through itself. It does not refer to an infinite spatial manifold or temporal manifold, which are distinct from a pure act of existing through itself. Infinite extension (space) and distension (time) has the sense of "continuing forever," but "unrestricted" applied to a pure act of existing through itself indicates "the absence of spatial, temporal, and other restrictions in this act of existing." Though it is virtually impossible to visualize what a non-spatial and non-temporal act of existence would be like, we must acknowledge that a pure act of existing through itself must be the most fundamental form of reality—because every restriction would have to be caused by it (see step 5).

Step 4: A pure unrestricted act of existing through itself must be unique (one and only one)[68]

The basic proof may be set out in three premises:

> If there is to be multiplicity among reali
> ties there must be a difference between
> those realities.

---

68 For Aquinas's proof of this, see *Summa contra gentiles*, Book 1, chap. 42, par. 3.

> If there is to be differences among reali
> ties, at least one of those realities must
> be restricted.
>
> But there can be no restriction in the pure
> act of existing through itself (see step
> 3).
>
> Therefore, there cannot be more than
> one pure act of existing through itself
> (*modus tollens*).

Explanation: The first premise is true *a priori*, because if there is no difference of any kind between two realities, they must be the self-same reality. Let us postulate two realities—X_1 and X_2. Now, let us suppose there is no difference between them—no difference as to space-time point, no difference in power or activity, no difference of qualities or characteristics, no difference whatsoever. What are they? Obviously, the same reality, and as such, there is only one.

The second premise is also true *a priori*. Think about it. If there is going to be a difference between, say, X_1 and X_2 (so there can be a multiplicity of them), then one of them will have to be something or have something or be somewhere or be in some other dimension that the other one is not. Let's suppose that X_1 has something that X_2

does not have. This means that X_2 is restricted or limited because it lacks this quality or characteristic. Similarly, if one postulates that X_1 is something that X_2 is not, then X_2 would again have to be limited (as manifest by its lack of that "something"). The same would hold true if X_1 was somewhere that X_2 was not, and if X_1 were in another dimension that X_2 was not. In short, every differentiating factor will entail a restriction of at least one of the differentiated realities.

The third premise has already been proven in step 3 ("But there can be no restriction in a pure act of existing through itself"); therefore, there cannot be a difference between two (hypothetical) pure acts of existing through themselves (*modus tollens*), meaning that there cannot be a multiplicity of pure acts of existing through themselves (*modus tollens*).

Let us see how this works: suppose that there are two pure acts of existing; then by the first premise, there will have to be some difference between act of existing₁ and act of existing₂. Recall that if there are no differences whatsoever between them, then they would be the self-same reality (one reality). Now if there is a difference between them, then one of them will have to have something, be something, be somewhere, or be in another dimension that the other one is not. If one of the pure acts of existing is restricted as to what it is (its way of existing), or where it is (its space-time point or its dimension), then it could not be unrestricted. As we saw in step 3, a pure act of existing through itself must be completely unrestricted (otherwise there would be something in it that did not exist through itself, and would have to be caused). In sum, every hypothetical act of existing$_2$ would have to have some kind of restriction which could not exist through itself, and would therefore have to be caused. This second pure act of existence therefore could not really be a *pure* act of existing through itself (a completely uncaused cause). Therefore, there can only be one pure act of existing through itself (and only one uncaused cause).

Step 5: The one pure act of existing through itself must be the ultimate cause (Creator) of all else that is[69]

This is derived from a two-step argument:

> As we have seen, an uncaused cause must be a pure unrestricted act of existing through itself, and there can only be

69 For Aquinas's discussion of this, see *Summa theologica* I, qu. 44, art. 1.

one pure unrestricted act of existing through itself, meaning that there can only be one uncaused cause in all reality.

If there can only be one uncaused cause in all reality, then the rest of reality must be caused (brought into existence).

Therefore, the one uncaused cause must be the ultimate cause of the existence of everything in reality besides itself. This is what is meant by the term "Creator."

Step 6: The one unrestricted act of existing through itself is transtemporal[70]

As we saw in step 3, a pure unrestricted act of existing is not subject to a temporal manifold

70 St. Augustine wrestled with this in Book 11 of the *Confessions*, coming to the conclusion that God is "an eternal now," and that he was not before time, because he was not in time (and that there was no time before time)—see particularly Book 11, chap. XIII, par. 16. Of course, he meant this *analogously*, because the best any of us can do is a negative judg-

because a temporal manifold would be different from it and would therefore have to be created by it. This means that the *pure* act of existing

ment—an act of existing which is not subject to a temporal manifold. Aquinas follows Augustine in the timelessness of God (as "eternal now"), and goes further, attempting to explain how such a timeless reality could understand "all time" of created realities that are conditioned by and progressing in time. He uses *analogies* to discuss this (such as seeing the progression of time from on high in a single vision or being at the center of a circle and observing all equidistant points at once), but we cannot think that he believed these analogies to represent *God's* reality, for they would imply that God's reality is conditioned by space and geometry, and also imply "eternalism" in which the past, present, and future coexist (a theory to which Aquinas did not subscribe). See *Compendium theologiae*, chap. 133 and *De veritate*, qu. 11, art. 12, resp. So we are back to the negative judgment that God is *not* conditioned by time, and that the whole of temporal reality (such as our universe and any other temporal reality beyond it) exists as a single *transtemporal* "thought" in God's unrestricted act of thinking (see Step 7). For a contemporary understanding of time and transtemporality (in light of Bergson and others), see Spitzer 2000, pp. 260–76; see also Spitzer 2010, pp. 183–96; see also Bergson 1965.

through itself is more fundamental than a temporal manifold, and that the temporal manifold is a creation—like a thought in the mind of a timeless and unrestricted act of mentation (see step 7).

We must acknowledge at the outset that a timeless act of mentation is impossible to visualize because, as many philosophers have noticed, our experience and imagination are conditioned by space and time. So how can we conceive of something we cannot imagine (picture think)? We can only do this by a kind of *via negativa*—that is by a conceptual process which avoids the temporalizing dimension of the imagination (picture thinking). We will have to avoid trying to "get a picture of it" and rest content with a negative judgment, namely, that there exists the pure unrestricted act of existing through itself which does *not* exist through a temporal manifold, nor through a spatial manifold, nor through anything else which is not itself. This pure act of existing must therefore be beyond any universe and any spatio-temporal reality, making it unimaginable. Nothing more can be said without distorting this reality through the conditions of our spatial and temporal imagination.

Step 7: The unrestricted act of existing through itself is an unrestricted act of mentation (thinking)[71]

What is thinking? A detailed explanation of this is given in my book, *New Proofs for the Existence of God: Contributions of Contemporary Physics and Philosophy* (chapter four). A brief outline must suffice here. Thinking (in contrast to imagining or picture thinking) is the grasp of relationships among realities—qualitative relationships, causal relationships, quantitative relationships, logical relationships, temporal relationships, spatial relationships, and any other intelligible relationship responding to the questions "what?", "where?", "why?", "when?", "how?", "how many?", and "how frequently?".

---

71 Aquinas's views here are expressed by Bernard Lonergan in *Verbum: Word and Idea in Aquinas* (Lonergan 1994, pp. 191–228). Aquinas first shows the spiritual nature of self-consciousness and thought in human beings (captured by chaps. 1 through 4 of Lonergan 1994) and then proceeds to use this as an analogy of God's completely simple, unrestricted act of self-consciousness (in chap. 5 of Lonergan 1994). The spiritual nature of human intellection is also captured by Lonergan's "notion of being" in Lonergan 1992, pp. 380–1 (see the reference below).

The ability to grasp relationships presumes some underlying unity through which the differences among realities can be related. For example, a map can unify diverse geographical locations so that they can be seen *in relation* to one another. A clock provides a unity for different times so that they may be seen in relationship to one another. There must be some underlying unity to bring together causes and effects in causal relationships. The same holds true for "what?" or "how?" or "how many?", etc. We might summarize by saying that thinking is a unifying act that sets differing realities or ideas into relationship with one another. Therefore, thinking goes beyond imagination (picture thinking that is limited to mere identification of individual things). When realities or ideas are set into relationship with one another, we can detect similarities and differences, quantities and causes, relative location and time, and we can even detect relationships among relationships. The pure act of existing through itself has no spatial, temporal, or other intrinsic restrictions. Therefore, there is nothing to prevent it from being in a perfectly transparent and reflective relationship to itself. This can be analogically understood by our own act of self-consciousness in which the same act of consciousness is both "grasper" and "grasped" simultaneously. This does not imply that our thinking has distinct parts, but rather that the one indivisible act of consciousness has *relational* differences "within" itself.[72]

Let us return now to the pure unrestricted act of existing through itself. Inasmuch as it is perfectly self-transparent, it can be perfectly present to itself as "grasper" and "grasped." This means it is perfectly self-conscious (in a fundamental unity without parts). The absence of spatial, temporal, and all other restrictions makes the one act of existing through itself perfectly self-transparent, perfectly self-relational, and therefore, perfectly present to itself and perfectly self-conscious.

Embedded in this self-consciousness is an awareness of the *difference* between itself as grasper and grasped, and so there is not only an awareness of self, but an awareness of relational *differences* within itself. Once "self" and

72 The term "within" here has no spatial connotation for obvious reasons; it refers only to the relational difference between "grasping" and "being grasped" in a single act of consciousness.

"difference" are grasped, all other ideas can be generated. The self can grasp not only itself, but what is different from itself—restriction and change. By grasping "self," "difference," "restriction," and "change," it can then generate the whole range of finite intelligibility.[73]

Notice that this unrestricted act of mentation is not like a brain or anything material or restricted. It is the essence of the pure unrestricted act of existing through itself. We cannot visualize it or imagine it; we can only *understand* that there must exist the one unrestricted act of existence through itself, and that it must be a perfect unity in relation to itself, and therefore, perfectly self-conscious and perfectly conscious of everything that could be different from it (the whole domain of finite intelligibility). Bernard Lonergan comes to a similar conclusion in his work *Insight: A Study of Human Understanding*, and calls the first

73 Plato, in his famous late dialogue *The Sophist*, recognized how the entire domain of restricted intelligibility could be generated and explained it through the interrelationship of six fundamental ideas (three diads): being and nonbeing, sameness and difference, and motion and rest. See Plato 1961, pp. 978–1028 (236d–264b).

cause "an unrestricted act of understanding understanding itself."[74] Inasmuch as the pure unrestricted act of existing through itself is an unrestricted act of thinking, it can design and create the entire world of finite being.

Dawkins's analysis in *The God Delusion* indicates no understanding of how an unrestricted act of existing can be self-transparent, self-relational, self-conscious, and therefore, capable of thinking and creating. He assumes that the more comprehensive the act of thinking, the more complex a reality must be. But this is true only for materialistic conceptions of thought which are based on "Turing machines" (the foundational mechanism for all computational machines and artificial intelligence). It does not include *nonmaterial* views of thinking which are based on the idea of unities (instead of aggregates) and upon self-transparency (instead of building blocks of mechanistic switches). Though non-materialistic views of thinking were accepted by ancient and medieval philosophers, the materialistic revolution (implicit in the natural sciences) closed the human imagination to this

74   Lonergan 1992, pp. 657–708.

possibility until Gödel's theorem and the quantum revolution perforce reopened it.[75] Bernard Lonergan and other contemporary philosophers were able to combine the ancient and medieval insight with the scientific and quantum revolutions, and so their assessment of mind is important for resolving contemporary paradoxes in artificial intelligence and the unexplained creativity of human intelligence.[76]

75 Gödel's theorem gave the first modern clue to the non-mechanistic and non-algorithmic dimension of human consciousness (Gödel 1931, pp. 173–98). Later John Lucas (1961, p. 120) and Roger Penrose (1989 and 1994, pp. 7–59) combined this insight with developments in quantum theory. Stephen Barr has an excellent summary of Gödel, quantum theory, and the transphysical dimension of human intelligence (Barr 2003, p. 214). I have written an explanation of the transphysical notion of thinking (in light of Lonergan's notion of being, quantum theory, and Gödel's theorem) in Spitzer 2010 (b), pp. 5–27.

76 See Lonergan's assessment of the notion of Being in *Insight: A Study of Human Understanding*: "[T]he notion of being penetrates *all* cognitional contents. It is the supreme heuristic notion. *Prior* to every content, it is the notion of the *to-be-known* through that content. As each content emerges, the 'to-be-known

Step 8: The pure unrestricted act of existing through itself must be absolutely simple (the absence of complexity)[77]

Basic Argument:

> Complexity entails parts.
> Parts entail restriction.
> But there can be no restriction in the pure act of existing through itself.
> Therefore, there can be no parts and no complexity in the pure act of existing through itself (*modus tollens*).

Explanation: The first and second premises are true *a priori*. Anything which is complex must have parts constituting a greater whole. Now if

> through that content' passes without residue into the 'known through that content.' Some blank in *universal anticipation* is filled in, not merely to end that element of anticipation, but also to make the filler a part of the anticipated. Hence, *prior* to all answers, the notion of being is the notion of the *totality* to be known through all answers" (Lonergan 1992, pp. 380–1; italics mine).

77 Aquinas articulated this in many different ways and works. A particularly clear passage may be found in *Summa theologica* I, qu. 3, art. 7.

there are parts constituting a greater whole, the parts must be more restricted than the whole (by definition), and therefore the parts must have restrictions as to their time, space, or way of existing. The proof of the third premise ("there can be no restriction in the pure act of existing through itself") was given in step 3. By *modus tollens*, if there can be no restrictions in the pure act of existing through itself, then there can be no parts in the pure act of existing through itself, and if no parts, then no complexity. It must be absolutely simple.

C. Response to Dawkins

As I noted in the introduction to this section, Dawkins contended that every designer would have to be more complex than what it designs, and from this he concludes that every designer must be more improbable than what it designs, because more complexity is always more improbable. We now see that Dawkins's unawareness of three pillars of logical and metaphysical thought led almost inevitably to his materialistic view of thinking (and his denial of "a designer"):

1. the necessity of an uncaused cause which must exist through itself alone (and must therefore be a pure act of existing through itself);

2. the necessity that a pure act of existing through itself be unrestricted and unique;

3. the consequence that this unique uncaused cause also be perfectly self-transparent, self-relational, self-present, and self-conscious.

Dawkins's materialistic view of thinking and causation is quite gratuitous in light of the developments in the philosophy of mathematics (from the time of Gödel to the present) and quantum theory (particularly violations of the Bell Inequality). These developments lead back to the remarkable logical and metaphysical simplicity revealed and demonstrated by St. Thomas Aquinas.

There is one more consequence of Dawkins's "errors of omission," namely, that he has provided yet another piece of evidence in favor of an intelligent Creator. For if one acknowledges that an uncaused cause (a pure unrestricted act of existing through itself which is perfectly self-conscious) must be absolutely simple (the absence of complexity), then by the second premise of his argument ("whatever is more complex is more improbable"), he proves that an uncaused cause would have to be *the most probable reality of all.* This fits very nicely with the necessity of an uncaused cause proved by Aristotle and Aquinas (step 1).

D. A Metaphysics of Restricted Being

After Aquinas proves the existence of God in the *De ente et essentia* (chapter four), he uses the metaphysical categories derived from his proof to shed light on the nature of restricted beings (chapter five). His conclusions may be summarized as follows: there must be two dimensions to every *restricted* reality—an act of existing (which causes beings to exist) *and* the restrictions to it (spatial, temporal, and particular *ways* of existing).

We can now understand what St. Thomas means by "an act of existing"—"the existence arising out of the ultimate causation of the one pure act of existing through itself." In step 5 of the proof, it was shown that there could only be one pure act of existing through itself, and that all other realities (besides this one) could not exist through themselves and would have to *ultimately* be caused (brought into being) by the one un-caused cause. Notice that the word "ultimately" here allows for proximate causes of being which are not the uncaused cause. For example, a cat might have formal and material causes of its ex-istence (such as cells and structures of cells), and those cells, in turn, might have formal and mate-rial causes such as molecules and structures of molecules, and those molecules in turn have for-mal and material causes such as atoms and struc-tures of atoms, etc. But all these formal and material causes are *not* the one act of existing through itself, so they cannot be the *ultimate* cause of the cat's existence. Why? Because they also have to be caused in order to exist. There-fore, the one uncaused cause must *ultimately* cause the existence of the cat even though it does so through thousands of proximate formal and material causes that are themselves "caused causes."

There can be no reality which is restrictions alone—there must be *something* which is re-stricted—and that "something" is an act of ex-isting (which causes the existence of those restrictions—whether they be spatial, temporal, or particular ways of acting). A square object is not merely the limitations of square (four equal sides and four inscribed right angles)—it is *something* (in reality or in a mind) which *has* the restrictions of "four equal sides and four inscribed right angles." An electron is not reducible to its restriction (attracting protons and repelling other electrons)—it is a *reality* which is restricted to attracting protons and repelling other electrons at particular magnitudes. Notice then that a restricted reality is not reducible to its restrictions—there must be *something* (an act of existing) which enables those restrictions to exist.

Interestingly, Stephen Hawking seems to have recognized this in his book *A Brief History of Time* when he wrote:

> Even if there is only one possible unified theory, it is just a set of rules and equations. What is it that breathes fire into the equations and makes a universe for them to describe? ... If we do discover a complete theory, ... we shall all ... be able to take part in the discussion of the question of why it is that we and the universe exist. If we find the answer to that, it would be the ultimate triumph of

human reason—for then we should know the mind of God.[78]

Hawking seems to recognize that the equations of physics describe only a set of *parameters* (limits such as maximums, minimums, and ratios of interaction) describing the *particular* actions and interactions of physical reality in space and time. They do not explain the *existence* of these parameters. The existence of physical reality is one thing and the equations of physics which describe its parameters are something different. They are unified with each other, but they are two different dimensions of physical reality. In the language we use above, there is the dimension of the act of existing ("what breathes fire into the equations" of physics) and the restrictions to existence (the parameters or equations of physics). This insight coincides with the Thomistic principle that "existence precedes essence." "Existence" refers to the act of existing (like Hawking's "what breathed fire into the equations"). "Essence" refers to the restrictions (such as space, time, and ways of existing) that underlie, not only the

78   Hawking 1988, pp. 174–5.

equations of physics, but all of the constituents and structures of the finite world.[79]

Now let us return to an act of existing through itself. The pure act of existing through itself cannot have a restricted essence, because a restricted essence is different from it. This means that every restricted essence cannot exist through itself and must therefore be caused by the one pure act of existing through itself. This also means that a pure act of existing through itself must be *prior to* any restricted essence, because it would have to exist in a *pure* state prior to causing any restricted essence. For this reason, Thomists insist that existence must precede restricted essence.

This metaphysics of restricted being lays a foundation for understanding physical reality— the very reality that constitutes the universe and would also have to constitute a multiverse or

79 Thomists called these restrictions "essence" because they make finite beings imaginable and intelligible to restricted acts of intellection (as human beings have). The interrelationship among limits, parameters, maximums, minimums, quantitative dimensions, and qualitative ways of existing allow a restricted act of understanding to grasp similarities and differences among various realities.

universe in the higher dimensional space of string theory (if these hypothetical structures really do exist). Physical reality, then, is an act of existing that is restricted by spatial manifolds, temporal manifolds, and restricted ways of existing (all of which exist through the ultimate causative action of the one pure act of existing through itself). In contrast to this, the one pure act of existing through itself is unrestricted, and therefore, transtemporal and transpatial. It is also an unrestricted act of thinking that is evidently transphysical. Physical and materialistic (spatio-temporal) ways of explaining thought and causation must therefore be avoided when explaining the thought and causation of the one pure act of existing through itself. The best descriptions we can achieve will have to be either analogies or negative judgments (explained in step 7).

VIII.

Conclusion: Combining the Physical and Metaphysical Evidence

In this essay we have discussed four kinds of evidence for the existence of an intelligent Creator:

1. space-time geometry proofs for a beginning of physical reality (implying a causative power transcending physical reality);

2. the evidence from entropy for a beginning of our universe (and physical reality) implying a causative power transcending physical reality;

3. the fine-tuning of the initial conditions and constants of the universe at the Big Bang (implying supernatural intelligence);

4. a logical-metaphysical proof for the

existence of a unique unrestricted pure act of existing through itself which is an unrestricted act of thinking and the Creator of all else that is.

Each of these four kinds of evidence has probative force in its own right (independently of the others). But when they are combined, they become complementary because they corroborate each other while emphasizing different dimensions of the one transcendent intelligent Creator.

John Henry Newman termed such a network of complementary evidence an "informal inference,"[80] that is, a conclusion reached by considering the accumulation of converging antecedent probable data sets. For Newman, truth claims did not have to be grounded in an infallible source of evidence or in a strictly formal deduction. They could be grounded in the convergence (complementarity and corroboration) of a multiplicity of *probabilistic* evidential bases. Certitude is not grounded in one base alone, but in a multiplicity of likely or probable evidential *bases*. Thus, even if one (or more) of these bases undergoes modification, the certitude intrinsic to the convergence remains intact (though it may be lessened).

80   Newman 1992, pp. 259–342 (chap. 8).

Our conclusion then is that both physical and philosophical evidence lead to the high probability of a unique, unrestricted, intelligent Creator. Space-time geometry proofs and entropy give *physical* and *scientific* evidence for a transcendent power creating our universe (and even a hypothetical multiverse or universe in the higher dimensional space of string theory). The evidence of the fine-tuning of initial conditions and constants of our universe complements the evidence of a creation by providing *physical* and *scientific* evidence of intelligence. In combination, they support the existence of a highly intelligent creative force of physical reality. The Thomistic metaphysical argument for a "unique, unrestricted, absolutely simple, pure act of existing through itself which is the Creator of all else that is and is a perfect act of thinking" gives logical-metaphysical evidence for an intelligent Creator, and so corroborates the evidence of physics. Yet it goes far beyond this by showing the necessity of an uncaused cause which must be a pure act of existing through itself. Since a pure act of existing through itself must be unrestricted and unique, the logical-metaphysical evidence goes beyond the physical evidence (which does not show either of these two attributes). The logical-metaphysical evidence also shows that this Being must be transphysical (transtemporal and trans-spatial), and in the absence of any spatio-temporal restrictions, must be completely self-transparent and self-relational making it perfectly present to itself, perfectly self-conscious, and capable of detecting everything different from itself (the entire world of finite intelligibility). In my view, this "informal inference" represents the true vision not only of John Henry Newman, but also of St. Thomas Aquinas and Monsignor Georges Lemaître, showing the comprehensiveness and depth of the Catholic intellectual tradition.

Bibliography

Aguirre, Anthony, and Steven Gratton. 2002. "Steady State Eternal Inflation." *Physical Review* D 65:083507.

Alabidi, Laila, and David Lyth. 2006. "Inflation Models and Observation." *Journal of Cosmology and Astroparticle Physics* 0605:016 (arXiv:astro-ph/0510441).

Aquinas, St. Thomas. 1947. *The Summa theologica of St. Thomas Aquinas*, vol. 1, trans. Fathers of the English Dominican Province (New York: Benziger Brothers).

———. 1965. *Aquinas on Being and Essence*, trans. Joseph Bobik (Notre Dame, Ind.: University of Notre Dame Press).

———. 1968. *On Being and Essence*, trans. Armand Maurer. 2nd rev. ed. (Toronto: Pontifical Institute of Mediaeval Studies).

———. 1991. *Summa contra gentiles*, Book One, trans. Anton C. Pegis (Notre Dame, Ind.: Notre Dame University Press).

Aristotle. 1980. *Aristotle's Physics*, trans. Hippocrates G. Apostle (Grinnell, Ia.: Peripatetic Press).

———. 1984. *Metaphysics*, trans. W. D. Ross. In *The Complete Works of Aristotle*, vol. 2, ed. Jonathan Barnes (Princeton: Princeton University Press).

Armitage, Angus. 1990. *Copernicus, the Founder of Modern Astronomy* (New York: Dorset Press).

Augustine, Saint. 1991. *Confessions*, trans. Henry Chadwick (New York: Oxford University Press).

Banks, Tom. 2007. "Entropy and Initial Conditions in Cosmology." *High Energy Physics—Theory*, arXiv:hep-th/0701146.

Banks, Tom, Michael Dine, and Elie Gorbatov. 2004. "Is There a String Theory Landscape?" *High Energy Physics—Theory*, arXiv:hep-th0309170.

Barr, Stephen M. 2003. *Modern Physics and Ancient Faith* (Notre Dame, Ind.: University of Notre Dame Press).

Bergson, Henri. 1965. *Duration and Simultaneity*, trans. Leon Jacobson (Indianapolis, Ind.: Bobbs-Merrill).

Borde, Arvind, Alan Guth, and Alexander Vilenkin. 2003. "Inflationary Spacetimes Are Not Past-

Complete." *Physical Review Letters* 90:151301 (arXiv:gr-qc/0110012).

Borde, Arvind, and Alexander Vilenkin. 1994. "Eternal Inflation and Initial Singularity." *Physical Review Letters* 72:3305–08.

———. 1997. "Violation of the Weak Energy Condition in Inflating Spacetimes." *Physical Review* D56:717–23 (arXiv:gr-qc/9702019).

Bradley, Walter L. 1998. "Designed or Designoid?" In *Mere Creation: Science, Faith and Intelligent Design*, ed. William A. Dembski (Downers Grove, Ill: InterVarsity Press), 33–50.

Breuer, Reinhard. 1991. *The Anthropic Principle: Man as the Focal Point of Nature* (Boston: Birkhauser).

Block, David L. 1992. *Our Universe: Accident or Design?* (Wits, South Africa: Star Watch).

Carroll, Sean. 2007. "Against Bounces." *Discover Magazine* (2 July 2007), http://blogs.discover-magazine.com/cosmicvariance/2007/07/02/against-bounces/.

Carter, Brandon. 1974. "Large Number Coincidences and the Anthropic Principle in Cosmology." In *Confrontation of Cosmological Theories with Observational Data: Symposium*, ed. M. S. Longair (Boston: D. Reidel), 291–8.

————. 2007. "The Significance of Numerical Coincidences in Nature." *High Energy Physics—Theory*, arXiv:0710.3543.

Collins, Robin. 2003. "Evidence for Fine-Tuning." In *God and Design: The Teleological Argument and Modern Science*, ed. Neil A. Manson (New York: Routledge), 178–99.

————. 2007. "How to Rigorously Define Fine-Tuning," http://home.messiah.edu/~rcollins/ Fine-tuning/ft.htm.

————. 2009. "The Teleological Argument: An Exploration of the Fine-Tuning of the Universe." In *The Blackwell Companion to Natural Theology*, ed. William Lane Craig and M. P. Moreland (Oxford: Blackwell), 202–81.

Craig, William Lane. 1993 (a). "The Finitude of the Past and the Existence of God." In William Lane Craig and Quentin Smith, *Theism, Atheism, and Big Bang Cosmology* (Oxford: Clarendon Press), 3–76.

————. 1993 (b). "The Caused Beginning of the Universe." In William Lane Craig and Quentin Smith, *Theism, Atheism, and Big Bang Cosmology* (Oxford: Clarendon Press), 141–60.

————. 2009. "Vilenkin's Cosmic Vision: A Review Essay of *Many Worlds in One: The Search for*

Other Universes." *Philosophia Christi* 11(1):232–8.

Craig, William Lane, and James D. Sinclair. 2009. "The *Kalam* Cosmological Argument." In *The Blackwell Companion to Natural Theology*, ed. William Lane Craig and J. P. Moreland (Malden, Mass.: Wiley-Blackwell), 101–201.

Davies, Paul. 1977. *Space and Time in the Modern Universe* (Cambridge: Cambridge University Press).

———. 1982. *The Accidental Universe* (Cambridge: Cambridge University Press).

———. 1983. *God and the New Physics* (New York: Simon and Schuster).

Davies, Paul, and Julian Brown,. 1988. *Superstrings: A Theory of Everything?* (Cambridge: Cambridge University Press).

Dawkins, Richard. 2008. *The God Delusion* (New York: Mariner Books).

DeMarco, Donald. 1986. "The Dispute between Galileo and the Catholic Church." *The Homiletic and Pastoral Review* 101:3 (May 1986): 23–51 and 101:4 (June 1986): 53–9.

Dine, Michael. 2004. "Is There a String Theory Landscape? Some Cautionary Notes." *High Energy Physics—Theory*, arXiv:hep-th/0402101v2.

Eddington, Sir Arthur. 1928. *The Nature of the Physical World* (Cambridge: Cambridge University Press).

Einstein, Albert. 1945. *The Meaning of Relativity* (Princeton: Princeton University Press).

———. 1956. *Lettres à Maurice Solovine* (Paris: Gauthier-Villars).

———. 1961. *Relativity: The Special and the General Theory*, trans. Robert W. Lawson (New York: Crown Publishers).

———. 1998. *The Collected Papers of Albert Einstein*, trans. Anna Beck (Princeton: Princeton University Press).

Gilson, Étienne. 1956. *The Christian Philosophy of St. Thomas Aquinas*, trans. Laurence K. Shook (New York: Random House).

———. 1960. *The Christian Philosophy of Saint Augustine*, trans. L. E. M. Lynch (New York: Random House).

Gingerich, Owen. 2000. "Do the Heavens Declare." In *The Book of the Cosmos*, ed. Dennis Richard Danielson (Cambridge, Mass.: Perseus Publishing), 524–5.

Gödel, Kurt. 1931. "Über formal unentscheidbare Sätze der Principia Mathematica und verwandter Systeme I." *Monatshefte für Mathematik und Physik* 38:173–98.

Gordon, Bruce. 2010. "Inflationary Cosmology and the String Multiverse." In Robert J. Spitzer, *New Proofs for the Existence of God: Contributions of Contemporary Physics and Philosophy* (Grand Rapids, Mich.: Eerdmans), 75–102.

Grossman, Lisa. 2012. "Why Physicists Can't Avoid a Creation Event." *New Scientist* 2847 (11 January 2012), http://www.newscientist.com/article/mg21328474.400.

Guth, Alan H. 1997. *The Inflationary Universe: The Quest for a New Theory of Cosmic Origins* (Reading, Mass.: Addison-Wesley).

———. 1999. "Eternal Inflation." In *Cosmic Questions, April 14–16, 1999, Washington, D.C., organized by the Dialogue on Science, Ethics, and Religion of the American Association for the Advancement of Science* (arXiv:astro-ph/0101507).

———. 2001. "Time since the Beginning." In *Astrophysical Ages and Time Scales*, ed. Ted von Hippel, Chris Simpson, and Nadine Manset, Astronomical Society of the Pacific Conference Series 245 (Orem, Utah: Astronomical Society of the Pacific), 3–17 (arXiv:astro-ph/0301199).

———. 2003. "Looking Backward: Inflation and

the Beginning of the Universe." *In Ground-Based Astronomy in the 21st Century: A National Science Foundation Sponsored Symposium*, https://www.nsf.gov/news/mmg/mmg_disp.jsp?med_id=52181.

Hansen, Jens Morten. 2009. "On the Origin of Natural History: Steno's Modern, but Forgotten Philosophy of Science." In *The Revolution in Geology from the Renaissance to the Enlightenment*, ed. Gary D. Rosenberg (Boulder, Colo.: Geological Society of America), 159–78.

Hawking, Stephen. 1980. "Theoretical Advances in General Relativity." In *Some Strangeness in the Proportion*, ed. Harry Woolf (Reading, Mass.: Addison-Wesley), 145–52.

———. 1988. *A Brief History of Time: From the Big Bang to Black Holes* (New York: Bantam Books).

———. 1993. *Black Holes and Baby Universes, and Other Essays* (New York: Bantam Books).

Hawking, Stephen, and Leonard Mlodinow. 2010. *The Grand Design* (New York: Random House).

Hawking, Stephen, and Roger Penrose. 1970. "The Singularities of Gravitational Collapse and Cosmology." *Proceedings of the Royal Society of London* A 314:529–48.

Henig, Robin Marantz. 2000. *The Monk in the Garden: The Lost and Found Genius of Gregor Mendel, the Father of Genetics* (Boston: Houghton Mifflin).

Hilbert, David. 1964. "On the Infinite." In *Philosophy of Mathematics*, ed. Paul Benacerraf and Hilary Putnam (Englewood Cliffs, N.J.: Prentice-Hall), 134–51.

Holton, Gerald, and Yehuda Elkana. 1997. *Albert Einstein: Historical and Cultural Perspectives* (Princeton: Princeton University Press).

Hoyle, Sir Fred. 1951. *The Nature of the Universe* (New York: Harper).

———. 1981. "The Universe: Past and Present Reflections," *Engineering and Science* 45:2 (November 1981): 8–12.

———. 1983. *The Intelligent Universe* (New York: Holt, Rinehart and Winston).

Hubble, Edwin. 1929. "A Relation between Distance and Radial Velocity among Extra-Galactic Nebulae." *Proceedings of the National Academy of Sciences* 15:168–73.

Jastrow, Robert. 1977. *Astronomy: Fundamentals and Frontiers* (New York: Wiley).

Kauffman, Stuart A. 1993. *Origins of Order: Self-Organization and Selection in Evolution* (New York: Oxford University Press).

———. 1995. *At Home in the Universe: The Search for Laws of Self-Organization and Complexity* (New York: Oxford University Press).

Lemaître, Georges. 1950. *The Primeval Atom: An Essay on Cosmogony*, trans. Betty H. and Serge A. Korff (New York: Van Nostrand).

Linde, Andrei. 1986 (a). "Eternal Chaotic Inflation." *Modern Physics Letters* A1:81–5.

———. 1986 (b). "Eternally Existing Self-Reproducing Chaotic Inflationary Universe." *Physics Letters* B175:395–400.

———. 1998. "Quantum Creation of an Open Inflationary Universe." *Physics Review* D58:083514 (arXiv:gr-qc/9802038).

———. 2002. "Inflation and String Cosmology." *International Journal of Modern Physics* A17S1:89–104 (arXiv:hep-th/0107176).

Livio, Mario. 2011. "Lost in Translation: Mystery of the Missing Text Solved." *Nature* 479:7372 (10 November 2011), 171–3.

Lonergan, Bernard. 1974. *A Second Collection by Bernard J. F. Lonergan,* ed. William F. J. Ryan and Bernard J. Tyrrell (Philadelphia: Westminster Press).

———. 1992. *Insight: A Study of Human Understanding*, Collected Works of Bernard J. F. Lonergan 3, ed. Frederick E. Crowe and

Robert M. Doran (Toronto: University of Toronto Press).

———. 1994. *Verbum: Word and Idea in Aquinas*, Collected Works of Bernard J. F. Lonergan 2, ed. Frederick E. Crowe (Toronto: University of Toronto Press).

Lucas, John R. 1961. "Minds, Machines, and Gödel." *Philosophy* 36:112–27.

Maggiore, Michele, and Riccardo Sturani. 1997. "The Fine-Tuning Problem in Pre-Big Bang Inflation." *Physics Letters* B415:335–43 (arXiv:gr-qc/9706053).

Newman, John Henry. 1992. *An Essay in Aid of a Grammar of Assent* (Notre Dame, Ind.: University of Notre Dame Press).

Penrose, Roger. 1989. *The Emperor's New Mind* (Oxford: Oxford University Press).

———. 1994. *Shadows of the Mind* (Oxford: Oxford University Press).

Penzias, Arno A., and Robert W. Wilson. 1965. "A Measurement of Excess Antenna Temperature at 40^{80} Mc/s." *Astrophysical Journal* 142:419–21.

Plato. 1961. *The Collected Dialogues of Plato*, ed. Edith Hamilton and Huntington Cairns (Princeton: Princeton University Press).

Plotner, Tammy. 2011. "The Expanding Universe—Credit to Hubble or Lemaître?" *The Universe Today* (10 November 2011), http://www.universetoday.com/90862/the-expanding-universe-credit-to-hubble-or-lemaitre/.

Smolin, Lee. 2006. *The Trouble with Physics: The Rise of String Theory, the Fall of a Science, and What Comes Next* (New York: Houghton Mifflin).

Spitzer, Robert J. 1989. *A Study of the Nature of Objectively Real Time* (Ann Arbor, Mich.: U.M.I.)

———. 2000. "Definitions of Real Time and Ultimate Reality." *Ultimate Reality and Meaning* 23(3):260–7.

———. 2003. "Indications of Creation in Contemporary Big Bang Cosmology." *Philosophy in Science* 10:35–106.

———. 2010 (a). *New Proofs for the Existence of God: Contributions of Contemporary Physics and Philosophy* (Grand Rapids, Mich.: Eerdmans).

———. 2010 (b). "Why Is Human Self-Consciousness Different from Artificial Intelligence and Animal Consciousness?" *Ultimate Reality and Meaning* 33:5–27.

Steinhardt, Paul J. 1983. "In the Very Early Universe." In *Proceedings of the Nuffield Workshop, Cambridge, 21 June to 9 July, 1982*, ed. G. W. Gibbons, Stephen W. Hawking, and S. T. C. Siklos (Cambridge: Cambridge University Press), 251–66.

Steinhardt, Paul J., and Neil Turok. 2002. "Cosmic Evolution in a Cyclic Universe." *Physics Review* D65:126003 (arXiv:hep-th/0111098).

Susskind, Leonard. 2003. "The Anthropic Landscape of String Theory." *High Energy Physics—Theory* (arXiv:hep-th/0302219).

Topper, David. 2013. *How Einstein Created Relativity out of Physics and Astronomy* (New York: Springer).

Vilenkin, Alexander. 1983. "The Birth of Inflationary Universes." *Physics Review* D27:2848.

———. 2006. *Many Worlds in One: The Search for Other Universes* (New York: Hill and Wang).

Wallace, William. 1984. *Galileo and His Sources: The Heritage of the Collegio Romano in Galileo's Science* (Princeton: Princeton University Press).